GW00394461

CORAL REEFS
SECRET CITIES OF THE SEA

ANNE SHEPPARD

Published by the Natural History Museum, London

First published by the Natural History Museum,
Cromwell Road, London SW7 5BD

ISBN 978 0 565 09356 3

A catalogue record for this book is available from the British Library

10 9 8 7 6 5 4 3 2 1

Designed by Mercer Design, London
Reproduction by Saxon Digital Services
Printed in China by C&C Offset Printing Co., Ltd.

CONTENTS

FOREWORD

BY STEPHEN CATLIN, CHIEF EXECUTIVE OF CATLIN GROUP LIMITED

I admit I did not know very much about coral reefs in 2012 when Catlin Group Limited began its sponsorship of the Catlin Seaview Survey, a series of scientific expeditions to increase our knowledge of reefs globally.

However, I quickly learned that coral reefs are not only beautiful, but they are also very important. These reefs are really like secret cities of the sea, homes to a wide variety of species of undersea life. The loss of coral reefs would have a profound impact on our oceans and sea life. Furthermore, I also learned how important reefs are to humans. Hundreds of millions of people depend on coral reefs as a barrier against tropical cyclones. Reefs are a vital source of food. They even play a major role in pharmaceutical research.

In short, coral reefs are a vital part of our planet, but we do not know as much about reefs as we should. One thing we do know is that their long-term survival is under threat.

Catlin Group Limited decided to sponsor the Catlin Seaview Survey because, as an insurer, we need to know more about the risks that society will face in the future. The loss of coral reefs – and all the benefits they provide – is certainly a major risk. Scientists need more information about reefs to help minimize these threats, and we hope the Catlin Seaview Survey can help provide that knowledge.

Catlin is proud to join with the Natural History Museum in the exhibition Coral Reefs: Secret Cities of the Sea, to help people know more about coral reefs, both to enjoy their beauty but also to realize the important role they play as part of our environment.

OPPOSITE: A healthy coral reefscape as captured by the Catlin Seaview Survey team as part of their global survey of coral reefs. This is Osprey Reef in the Coral Sea, 110 km (68 miles) northeast of the outer edge of the Great Barrier Reef, a UNESCO Marine World Heritage site.

INTRODUCING

THE CORAL REEF

RIGHT: A coral of the genus *Galaxea* showing the individual coral polyps in their limestone skeletons, with tentacles extended.

PREVIOUS PAGE: The reefs of Heron Island, which lies within the Great Barrier Reef Marine Park area. The island is the base for a large coral reef research station where much coral reef ecology research is carried out.

Coral reefs are beautiful and beguiling formations in the tropical seas. The first people to have a professional interest in coral reefs were mariners, for whom the complex reef systems in shallow water were always a hazard and the cause of the loss of a great many lives. Reefs were inaccessible and treacherous, hidden just beneath the water and difficult to map accurately. Even so, early scientists made often dangerous and heroic voyages to try to understand these vast, mysterious and beautiful structures. The reef flat, the part of the reef that becomes accessible at low tide, was the first to be studied, and it was here that the realization was first made that these rocky structures were made by animals. Biology and geology are very much connected in the study of coral reefs.

Coral reef systems are the richest, most diverse, habitat on Earth. They are often compared to the great tropical rainforests, which are the most biodiverse land habitats. They are home to more different phyla – groupings of related organisms such as molluscs, echinoderms or fish – than even the rainforests are. There are about 35 different phyla of animals on Earth and 32 of them are represented on coral reefs. All of them play a vital role in the very complex, interconnected, community that has its home there. Although the reefs cover less than 1% of the global marine environment, they support around 25% of all marine species. And for millions of people who live alongside them, they are crucial in many ways, from supplying essential food to protecting the coastlines. In addition, because they are also very beautiful, they provide very significant income from tourists.

The rocky foundations of these rich, stony, coral cities under the sea are built by tiny coral animals called polyps. Their skeleton is external and it is built of limestone, the constituents of which are extracted from the seawater, and laid down by the polyp, which lives in a small opening on the surface into which it can retract. It is these external skeletons that build the reefs.

The polyp has tentacles that it can extend out of the opening on the surface of the skeleton to catch food. It also photosynthesizes and carries out the various activities essential to life, such as respiration and digestion. Coral polyps are therefore the builders of the reef, and upon them all the other life on the reef depends. At the same time that corals build up the reef, various organisms and processes keep that growth in check, so that the reefs' net growth each year is relatively small. Sponges, molluscs, worms and many other reef inhabitants bore into the coral rock, either to create their own homes or to hunt and eat those that have already done so. Parrotfish, those large colourful reef fish with a beak to rival many avian parrots, bite the coral – limestone, polyps and all. The digested remains are excreted as a fine sand, which in turn is used by other organisms to cement together the reef again. It is all an intricate web of life, of growth and recycling.

LEFT: A large school of greenthroat parrotfish, *Scarus prasiognathos,* eating the coral and limestone. These fish are important in maintaining the health of the reef as they recycle nutrients and reef building materials.

RIGHT: Map showing the global distribution of coral reefs. The heavier the shading, the more coral species occur in that area.

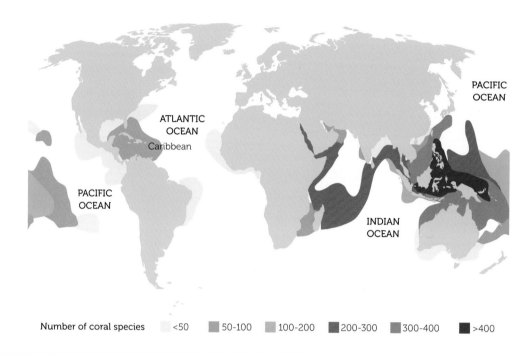

Number of coral species ▢ <50 ▢ 50-100 ▢ 100-200 ▢ 200-300 ▢ 300-400 ▢ >400

THE CORAL TRIANGLE

ABOVE: The Coral Triangle is the area of highest coral species diversity; radiating away from this locus, species numbers drop.

Coral reefs are renowned for their high biodiversity, yet around the world they show differing degrees of species richness. Within the vast Indo-West Pacific region lies an area that encompasses Indonesia, Malaysia, Papua New Guinea, the Solomon Islands, Timor-Leste and the Philippines. This area, of over 6 million km² (2.3 million miles²), contains about 30% of the world's coral reefs and is frequently referred to as the Coral Triangle. It stands out as having the most highly diverse coral reefs in the world, with over 500 species of reef-building corals (more than 75% of all known coral species) and over 2,000 species of reef fish. Iconic species abound, and seven of the eight turtle species occur there as well as the majestic whale shark, the rare coelacanth and a high diversity of other marine organisms. Over 120 million people living in the area are either directly or indirectly dependent upon the marine resources of the region. Fisheries exports produce over US$3 billion annually with another US$3 billion from tourism directly linked to the coastal resources.

Outside the Coral Triangle, there are between 200 and 500 coral species in the rest of the Indo-West Pacific region. The Caribbean reef region, which is much smaller and completely different in its coral species composition, is one of the lower biodiversity reef areas, with only about 60 coral species.

In areas at the edges of the conditions necessary for reef growth, such as at higher latitudes where the water is cooler, or areas that are isolated from main coral regions, such as West Africa, far fewer species of coral are found.

Warm tropical waters are necessary for the reef corals to grow, so the part of the world in which they are able to do so is limited to the warmer areas of the oceans, roughly between the tropics of Capricorn and Cancer, extending a little further towards higher latitudes where currents of warm water flow. They grow most profusely in waters with a temperature range between about 20 and 30 °C (68 and 86 °F). They also need light, so are found only in relatively shallow water, although corals have many closely related cousins that do not need light and so can live much deeper in the ocean.

There are two main coral reef regions of the world. The first is the vast Indo-Pacific region. This includes: the Indian Ocean with its numerous archipelagos, from Arabia to South Africa through to Southeast Asia, which is richest of all; both western Australia and eastern Australia, with its Great Barrier Reef; and the numerous coral island nations of the Pacific Ocean, all the way across to Panama. The second coral reef region is the Atlantic Ocean, mostly in the Caribbean, but with important extensions northward to Bermuda and south to Brazil.

Controls on reefs

Several natural factors limit where reefs grow. One is freshwater coming from rivers, as reefs require normal seawater salinity levels of about 3.5%. Breaks exist in reefs offshore from river mouths, and these have determined the location of many harbours in tropical areas, where the breaks in the reefs allowed ships access to the shore. The largest rivers, which carry huge volumes of freshwater down to the sea, prevent reefs forming over a very large area. The discharge from the great Amazon, for example, inhibits reef growth not only at its mouth but also for almost 3,000 km (1,865 miles) along the length of the coast. This Amazon barrier also stops most coral larvae from dispersing through it, so that many of the corals that grow off the coast of Brazil south of the Amazon are endemic and are not found in the adjacent Caribbean. Along with the fresh water are large amounts of sediment, which are equally inhibiting to the development of reefs.

BELOW: Freshwater and sediment from a huge watershed collect via many tributaries into the Amazon. All this discharges into the sea at about 200,000 m³ (7,300,000 ft³) per second.

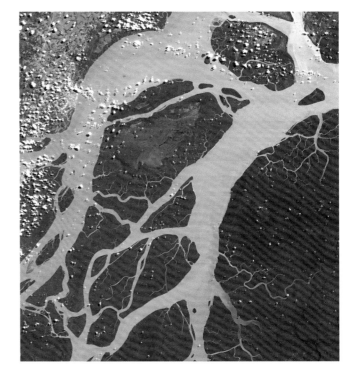

ABOVE: A very sedimented reef with dead and dying coral polyps at Fasht Adhm in the Persian Gulf. Corals are easily killed by fine sand, which smothers the delicate polyps.

Salinity, sedimentation and temperature are among the most important factors that control the distribution of reefs. These and other factors, such as freshwater, wave energy and light, also control which corals grow where on any particular reef. Different species of coral have varying degrees of tolerance to different environmental factors. As we have just seen, fresh water from rivers stops most species from growing, but a small river may stop only some corals from growing and allow other species that are more tolerant of reduced salinity to survive. Similarly, sediment in the water affects species differently, some being more tolerant to the sediment and so able to thrive when other species cannot. The advantage to the coral of developing a tolerance to one or other factor is that it has far less competition for space in which to grow on these areas of reef. This is comparable, for example, to drought-tolerant plants growing in arid areas, where there is far less competition for space than in a rainforest.

Wave energy is another factor to which different coral species have different degrees of adaptation. Fragile, delicately branched corals are less able to withstand the high wave energies that pound the edges and shallowest parts of the reef, and so these grow deeper

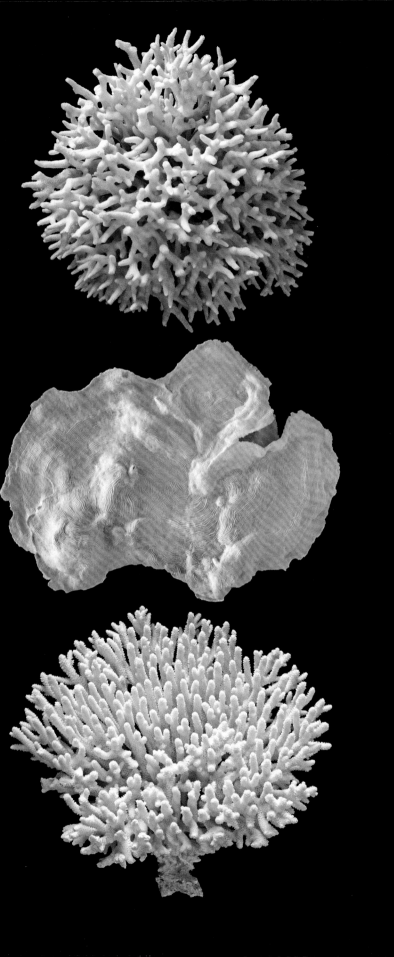

TOP LEFT: *Seriatopora caliendrum* has different growth forms depending on the wave exposure where it is growing. It has a more sturdy form in exposed locations and is more delicately and finely branched in sheltered locations.

ABOVE: A close up of a branch tip of *Seriatopora caliendrum* shows one of the key identification features of this genus. All the corallites are in regular rows down the length of the branch.

CENTRE LEFT: The flat *Pachyseris speciosa* is common on deeper parts of the reef where its plate-like shape allows it to collect as much light as possible, but this makes it susceptible to damage from sediment.

ABOVE: The tramline-like valleys of *Pachyseris speciosa,* with very small calices where the polyps live, are visible in this close up image. This genus of corals all have very small polyps in relation to the colony size.

BOTTOM LEFT: *Acropora millepora* lives in shallow water and is common on reef flats, or the shallow reef slope, throughout the Indo-Pacific. It is impacted by several different threats and is classified by IUCN as 'Near Threatened'.

down the reef slope, whereas sturdy boulder-shaped corals much more easily tolerate the frequent pounding from storm waves and so are able to survive these conditions higher up the reef slope. Light availability also decreases as you descend the reef, and so different corals have shapes adapted to maximize the use of the light available at different depths. As in all ecological situations there is a trade-off between living in the best, most advantageous, space and having to fight to stay there because many other species want to be there as well.

The shapes of reefs

The effect of many of these ecological controls on corals and their growth means that there is a typical pattern and shape to a reef. There are a few major types of reef (see page 60), but if we look at a typical reef around a coral island or along a shoreline we see a similar layout wherever in the world this coral island or shore exists. Firstly, extending from the shore is the reef flat. As the name suggests, this is a flat area of reef that can extend outwards anything from about 10 m (33 ft) to several hundred metres and is usually made of old eroded coral rock that has been planed level by waves. It is an area that usually has few coral species on it, as it is a difficult environment for corals, or indeed any organisms, to grow. It is a shallow area, at most a few metres deep, and at low tide can often become almost dry. This means its inhabitants have to be able to survive drying out at low tide, the addition of fresh water from rivers and rain, heat and ultraviolet radiation from the sun, and being bathed in warmer water for hours at a time, as well as predation from a new set of predators from the land. As a result, diversity here is generally fairly low.

At the seaward edge of the reef flat is the reef crest. This is the part of the reef that takes the brunt of the wave action, and is usually seen from the shore as a line of breaking white waves. From the sea, this line of white water is the warning to shipping of the presence of a reef. Some sturdy, small, compact corals grow here, but the wave energies can be very high during storms. Beyond the reef crest is deeper water, and here we are truly getting down into the realm of the living corals. Some reefs descend precipitously from the reef crest, but more typically a shallow, gently sloping reef terrace leads outwards for anything from about 10 m to 100 m (33 to 330 ft) or more. The reef terrace may take us down to depths of about 10 to 20 m (33 to 66 ft) deep. This area can be rich in corals and is the shallow reef area that people can see from boats, looking down into the colourful world of the coral reef below with its teeming, darting, reef fishes and other life.

OPPOSITE: Various coral shapes show the rich diversity and high coral cover of the shallow sunlit reef on Rinca Island, Komodo National Park, Indonesia. There are massive *Porites* sp., brain coral and *Acropora* sp. of table coral. There is fierce competition for space in this part of the reef, so individual corals are less likely to grow as big as they would in a less optimal habitat.

ABOVE The 'drop off', where a gently sloping shallow reef drops steeply down to deeper water on Sipadan Island, Sabah, Malaysia.

The deeper edge of this terrace is where there may be a steepening of the reef slope, often called the 'drop off'. For the diver, the swim over the drop off to the deeper slope reveals an extraordinary panorama that unfolds before them. Here the corals seem to cover most of the sea floor, with huge sea fans spreading their intricate branches out into the water. Fish of all sizes, shapes and colours dart or school among the corals, with the shyer fish looking out from under coral shelters. Large predatory fish swim in the deeper waters, and quick flashes of silver catch your eye as a fish, maybe a shark, catches a meal. There is an extraordinary busyness on a healthy reef.

There are variations of this theme. Some reefs are steep from near the surface, sometimes nearly vertical, whereas others slope more gently for a longer distance. But the general structure is the same because these are structures made by living animals and processes that respond in similar ways throughout the world.

This is the coral reef.

LEFT On the deeper parts of the reef where there is less light such as here in Manzamo, Okinawa, the sea fans catch their planktonic prey in their net-shaped branches, which spread out into the current.

Clear waters

There are few, if any, ecosystems where all the inhabitants are so well interconnected and integrated as they are on the reef. Coral reefs are hugely productive and produce vast amounts of biomass – the quantity of biological material. Yet tropical coral waters are oligotrophic – that is, they are poor in nutrients – compared with temperate or cold waters. Charles Darwin himself wondered how such nutrient-poor waters could sustain such a rich ecosystem.

That the water around a coral reef is poor in nutrients is the reason why tropical seas are so clear – the more nutrient-rich the water, the murkier it becomes. This is also the reason that tropical seas are so blue. Temperate and cold seas are green in colour because of the nutrients and organic matter in the water. How can the coral reef be so productive in such nutrient-poor waters? The answer is a complex one, but the basic

reason is that all the nutrients are very tightly recycled and kept within the reef system. Very little is lost or wasted on a coral reef.

It is no surprise to learn that this beautiful, highly biodiverse habitat is valued by those humans who live close to the reefs. Coral reefs provide valuable ecosystem services to people. For example, they provide large amounts of food, with many billions of dollars worth of fish caught globally on coral reefs every year, and in many developing countries artisanal gleaners collect many different organisms from shallow areas: octopuses and other molluscs, sea cucumbers, fish and seaweeds. The reef crest described above also stops the storm wave energy from eroding away infrastructure on the shore, such as roads, bridges and buildings. In addition, revenue from tourism provides substantial income and hard currency – most of it, in several cases – for many small or developing nations. So for ecological and economic reasons, coral reefs around the world are valuable assets for humanity.

LEFT: A top predator on the reef is the shark. This whitetip reef shark, *Triaenodon obesus*, is common on healthy, unfished reefs.

PREVIOUS PAGE: A shallow protected reef system at Wilson Reef on the Great Barrier Reef. The image shows a variety of hard, reef-building corals from the table-like *Acropora* sp. to the boulders of *Porites* sp., all of which provide habitat and protection for the myriad of creatures that live on the reef.

The huge structures that are coral reefs – for example, the Great Barrier Reef is the largest structure built by any living community of organisms on Earth – are, amazingly, built by tiny, soft-bodied coral polyps. Each coral 'head' is a single coral colony – a colonial organism composed of many genetically identical individuals. A single coral polyp may be a few millimetres to a few centimetres in diameter, depending on the species. It looks much like a sea anemone, and coral polyps and sea anemones are indeed closely related, along with the jellyfish – all have no backbone or any internal bones at all. In scientific nomenclature, these animals are all members of the phylum Cnidaria (pronounced with a silent 'c').

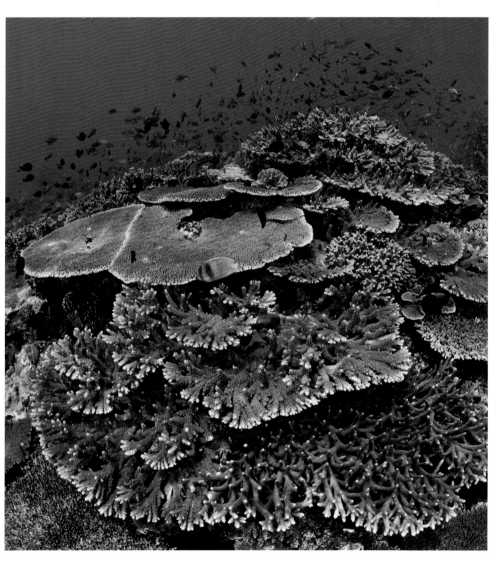

RIGHT: A reef is a three-dimensional structure allowing more than 1 m² (1 yard²) of life in each 1 m² (1 yard²) of substrate. This plate coral reefscape with damselfish and fairy basslets is in Komodo, Indonesia.

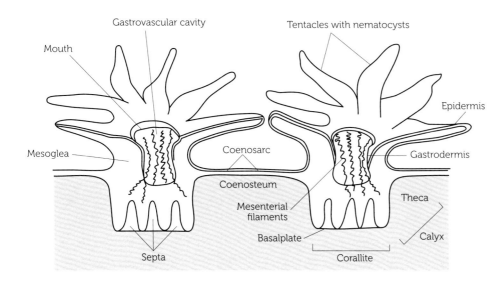

The polyp has a very simple construction of a ring of tentacles surrounding a mouth, which is at the top of a short, tube-like body. The interior of this body contains the stomach, into which food caught by the tentacles is passed directly, through the mouth. In the stomach the food is digested and the waste material expelled back out through the mouth. The body cavity is lined with structures called mesenteries, which create a large surface area, in the same way that the vanes on a radiator do. These mesenteries contain the specialized cells responsible for digestion and also the coral's reproductive organs. In many species there is a layer of tissue separating each polyp, called the coenosarc, which connects all the polyps to each other and allows them to share nutrients and the products of photosynthesis and respiration. The coensarc can also be used in communication to some degree as it contains a simple neural net; communication can be seen when the polyps in the whole colony progressively retract in a wave into the skeleton if some part of the colony is touched. In this way, although each polyp is an individual, in many senses the polyps work together as a single much larger organism.

Most people know about the jellyfish's ability to sting, sometimes fatally, and one of the criteria that groups jellyfish, sea anemones and corals together, is this ability to sting using specialized cells in the tentacles called nematocysts. These are used to capture prey and also to defend themselves against predators. The nematocysts consist of a cell with a coiled thread inside, at the end of which is a dart through which a toxin is injected. At the top of the nematocyst is a hair-like trigger which, when activated, shoots the

RIGHT: The stinging cell, or nematocyst, which a coral polyp uses to capture its prey is activated by a hair-like trigger, which when touched causes the release of the barb. According to recent research, the nematocyst can shoot out at G-forces of up to 5,410,000 g.

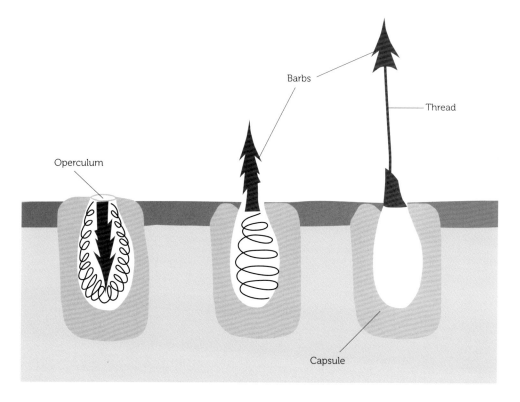

dart into whatever brushed against it. Corals have millions of these nematocysts on the surface of their tentacles, and they use them to catch zooplankton – small larvae and other organisms – and even tiny fish, which make up their food. Although some jellyfish, in particular the box jellyfish, have severe stings, coral nematocysts of most species are barely able to penetrate human skin and so are harmless to us, although in many cases the toxins can cause some irritation. A few species of coral relatives, such as the aptly named fire coral, are able to cause painful swelling, especially in delicate skin areas.

Close associations

Capturing tiny, floating prey is not the only feeding method employed by corals. They have an even more fascinating method, which arises from their close relationship with single-celled algae called zooxanthellae. The zooxanthellae and their host corals have a symbiotic relationship with each other, meaning that both benefit from the relationship. So interdependent are the two that reef-building corals cannot live without the zooxanthellae. The algae have the scientific name of *Symbiodinium*, and live within the coral tissue itself.

LEFT: Zooxanthellae are quickly recruited into new coral tissue as it grows. The white edge seen on these corals is new tissue into which zooxanthellae have not yet grown.

These algae photosynthesize, that is, they use energy from the sun to create food in the same way as other plants do. They then share this food with the coral in exchange for nutrients from the coral, with up to 95% of the products of their efforts going to the coral host.

This relationship between the coral and the zooxanthellae is vital in providing the corals with the energy, in the form of food, required to build their large limestone skeletons, which is very energetically demanding. It is only this energy input from the zooxanthellae that enables corals to do this at the rate they do, and this is ultimately fundamental to the building of the entire reef. The relationship with photosynthetic zooxanthellae explains why zooxanthellae corals must grow in the sunlit shallows, generally less than 60 m (around 200 ft) deep in clear water and much shallower in turbid water.

There are some coral species such as *Tubastraea* sp. (see page 26) that do not have this symbiotic relationship with zooxanthellae, and these are therefore much smaller and slower growing and do not contribute significantly to building the reef. Although several such species do live on reefs, commonly in darker locations such as caves, they are able to live in much deeper water throughout the oceans, because without symbiotic zooxanthellae they have no need for sunlight.

ZOOXANTHELLAE AND THEIR CLADES

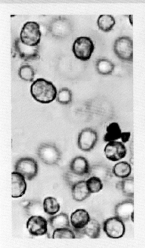

ABOVE: The zooxanthellae, *Symbiodinium* sp., are visible in the surface tissue of the coral polyp where they photosynthesize using the available sunlight.

LEFT: Close-up of zooxanthellae from a coral, showing the single-celled organisms that carry out the photosynthesis.

The reason corals are able to build huge reef structures is because of their symbiotic relationship with the zooxanthellae *Symbiodinium*. There are a number of *Symbiodinium* species, although those that live in corals are all thought to be one species. They are called dinoflagellates (from the Greek dinos, which means 'whirling' and flagellum, which means 'whip'). Zooxanthellae can live outside the coral, and in that state they are motile – that is, they use their flagellum to propel themselves – but inside the coral they lose the flagellum and the ability to move. Being algae, they contain chlorophyll and so photosynthesize. Several reef animals have zooxanthellae, such as some soft corals, anemones, flatworms and giant clams.

In the past, the genus was recognized to include more than one species, but it was difficult to distinguish them, although a few different species have been named. Using modern genetic sequencing techniques it has been discovered that there are distinct differences between some of them. These may in fact turn out to be different genera. At the moment, though, they are called clades, meaning that each has a distinct, ancient, genetic lineage. Clades A–H have been identified, each with physiological differences, mostly relating to their tolerance to light and water temperature.

Corals cannot tolerate seawater temperatures higher than about 30°C (86°F), above which they eject the zooxanthellae from their tissues. High light levels also induce this response. Coral tissues are mostly translucent, and it is the colour of the zooxanthellae that gives corals their predominant greenish-brown coloration. Each square centimetre of coral tissue contains approximately one million zooxanthellae, which means that there are one or two in each cell of coral tissue. Without the zooxanthellae in their tissues to add colour, the white limestone skeleton shines through and the corals become white. The term for this event is 'bleaching'.

Mass bleaching events are becoming increasingly common as seawater warms due to climate change (see page 92). An increase in temperature above the critical level, often coupled with an increase in light caused by calm water that allows more light to penetrate the sea surface, leads to a stressed relationship between the coral and it's zooxanthellae, which causes the zooxanthellae to be ejected. This can result in the death of the coral if it is prolonged. If, after a short period, the temperature drops again, the coral is able to re-recruit zooxanthellae back into its tissues. However, if it does not cool within a short time the coral will die through lack of food. The critical time varies and is dependent on how high the temperature is above normal. Commonly about a one degree rise for 10 weeks is fatal to corals.

Different clades of zooxanthellae are prevalent in different geographical regions because they are adapted to thrive in the different ecological conditions that exist in different locations. For example, Clade C is the most common globally, but Clade B is more common in Caribbean reefs. Clade D thrive better in areas where the water temperature is higher and perhaps more turbid, so they are more common in the Persian Gulf, whereas Clade A are more resistant to higher light intensities. In any one region – in fact in any single colony – several clades exist in different proportions, and there is hope that corals will be able to adapt slightly to warming sea temperatures by having different proportions of resistant clades in their tissues.

The symbiosis between corals and algae also explains one of the mysteries that perplexed biologists until the zooxanthellae were discovered: where is the primary production on the reef? All life is dependent on plants to convert sunlight into food – plants are the basis of the food chain. They are obvious in a forest or a meadow, and even in a temperate marine habitat with all its macro-algae (seaweed). But for years it was a mystery where the plants were to support all the life on a reef. There are some large seaweeds on a reef, and even some species that produce limestone to contribute to the reef growth, but nowhere near enough was visible to support all the life seen there. The symbiotic algal zooxanthellae are the answer: the plant life is there, it is just hidden away inside the corals.

OPPOSITE: Corals without photosynthetic zooxanthellae can live deeper on the reef where there is less sunlight, or in caves where light is dim. These *Tubastraea* sp. are growing well out of any sunlight. The tentacles are extended to catch their planktonic prey.

The calcareous skeleton laid down by the polyp is its home and protection. Each individual polyp lives in a small cup-like indentation within the colony called a corallite. At night, the polyp can extend its tentacles out of the corallite to catch food, and in the daytime it can retract them safely inside for protection from predators. To build the limestone skeleton, the polyp extracts calcium and carbonate from the seawater. The process of turning this into limestone is complex, and a side benefit of the process is that it releases carbon dioxide from the carbonate. Carbon dioxide is essential in the process of photosynthesis and is absorbed by the zooxanthellae.

There are several types of limestone, and that laid down by corals is a crystalline form called aragonite. Using a layer of specialized cells at the base of the polyp, this aragonite is laid down in the shape of a small cup to form the corallite. As it does so the polyp is raised up – and so the colony grows.

BELOW: A diagram showing the layout of the calcareous corallite, built by the coral polyp and within which it lives.

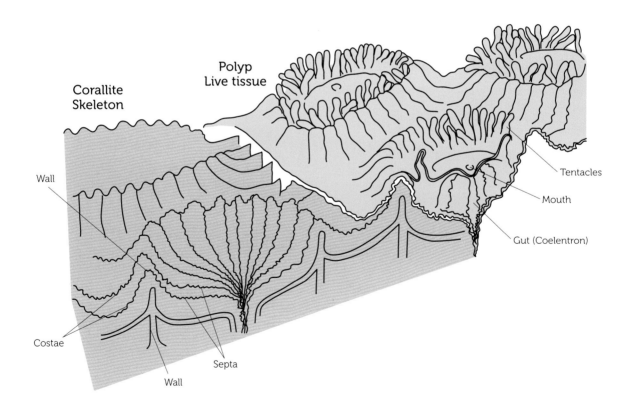

Corallite Skeleton

Polyp Live tissue

Wall

Tentacles

Mouth

Gut (Coelentron)

Costae

Septa

Wall

Coral reproduction

Corals can reproduce both sexually and asexually. Regarding sexual reproduction, most corals are hermaphrodite, which means that each colony produces both male and female gametes. A few species have separate male and female colonies and a few are known to change sex at different stages of life too.

In sexual reproduction, the majority of corals are broadcast spawners, releasing sperm and egg bundles into the water for external fertilization. Coral adults after all are sessile (attached to the substrate and unable to move from the spot where they first settled), so cannot come together to reproduce. The only way a species can successfully exchange genetic material is for both males and females to release eggs and sperm – collectively called gametes – into the water at the same time. The gametes from any one species are released simultaneously so that, with so many in the water at the same time, the chance is increased that a male and female gamete will meet to allow fertilization to take place. The resulting tiny, pear-shaped, fertilized larvae are called planulae which eventually settle in a part of the reef that might allow them space to grow. Once settled, the new corals have developed several strategies to allow them to compete with their neighbours for space (see page 33). For many, this early settlement becomes a battle for survival with polyps of neighbouring corals that could overgrow them.

Frequently, fascinating and important new discoveries are made in the world of coral reef research. In 1981, researchers in Australia discovered that corals reproduce in a mass spawning event, in which many species – and there are several hundred different ones – all spawn together over one or two nights. But why do so many unrelated species need to do this at the same time? Such large numbers of gametes are released that they form large slicks on the surface, and it is thought that because there are so many at the same time, predators are simply swamped. How do the corals arrange this mass event? The details are still not fully understood but the spawning takes place after sunset following a full moon. There are different cues which induce the maturation of the gametes, from length of day and temperature of the water, and the timing of the mass release is determined by the number of hours after sunset, amongst other factors that have not yet been resolved. In different places around the world the mass spawning takes place during different months: March in Western Australia, August in the Caribbean and October/November in the Great Barrier Reef.

RIGHT: An *Acropora* sp. coral in the process of releasing gametes into the water at Heron Island, Great Barrier Reef. Most of these gametes will become food for many reef inhabitants but enough will survive to start the next generation.

Divers who have been in the water to witness this event invariably call it spectacular, like a snowstorm of orange, pink, red and yellow gametes. On the surface the smell is strong, like a much stronger version of the normal smell of corals, with slicks so thick that it clogs the divers' hair as they leave the water.

Mass spawning of gametes is not the only method of sexual reproduction employed by corals. About a quarter of corals have internal rather than external fertilization and brood the planulae within their tissues. Here, only the male sperm are released into the water and then are taken in by the female coral. The fertilized eggs develop into planulae internally, and are released as free swimming larvae, which then swim out of the mouth of the polyp and into the water. This method of reproduction can take place over a much longer period than just the very few nights of the mass spawning.

After fertilization takes place, by whatever method, the tiny planulae swim in the water for varying lengths of time, depending on the species. This can be from a few hours to a few weeks, sometimes even longer as they already have their own complement of zooxanthellae which they obtained from their parent and so can feed right from the start. When ready to settle, the planula swims to the sea floor, finds a suitable place and metamorphoses into a tiny coral polyp, about 1 mm across. The planula has to find an empty space on which to settle and this can be very difficult to find on a busy reef where space to grow is at a premium, and a great many die at this stage. The coral has to grow quickly at first because it is very vulnerable to many different dangers. It may be eaten by one of many predators, a butterflyfish for example, or it may be overgrown by algae, or it may be killed by another coral as described later.

Corals also reproduce asexually. After a coral settles, it grows by budding, a process where each polyp divides thus expanding the colony, sometimes into colonies of millions of polyps reaching several metres across. This budding is an asexual division of the individual polyps and there are several ways this can happen (see page 37). This coral growth is fundamental to how a reef grows into such large structures.

There are various other ways that asexual colony propagation can work, such as when, particularly during a storm, fragments of the more fragile species of corals are broken off and rolled away. These may then attach and then grow to form whole new colonies. This fragmentation is not always accidental, some can deliberately fragment themselves into pieces that then grow into full-sized adults.

The many ways corals reproduce and grow, using various methods of reproduction and feeding, underpins the whole complex assortment of life that exists on the reef. Corals lay the foundation, both literally and metaphorically, for the huge variety of that life that is astonishing in its relationships and its complexity.

Coral interactions

Space is at a premium on a healthy reef, and finding room to grow can be a problem, especially as many of the inhabitants are sessile. In order to make more space to grow into, a slow but deadly battle takes place on the reef, mainly at night when the coral polyps have expanded out of their limestone corallites. This may seem difficult to imagine with seemingly unmoving, rocky corals, but many of them are able to kill adjacent corals of different species by one or more of four different methods.

All corals, like their cousins the jellyfish, have stinging cells called nematocysts in their tentacles. Most are barely able to penetrate human skin (except in the case of the related and aptly named fire coral) but are used to kill and capture small prey. Most corals such as *Galaxea* sp., *Euphyllia* sp. and *Favia* sp. can produce specialized tentacles called sweeper tentacles, named after their distinctive movement. These are much longer than normal tentacles and are packed with nematocysts. They sweep out over the neighbouring subordinate coral to sting and kill its tissue. The length of the sweeper tentacles has no correlation with the length of the coral's normal tentacles, and a coral with short regular tentacles can often produce much longer sweeper tentacles than those in many longer tentacled corals. This may illustrate the different needs each species has for a greater reach. These very long sweeper tentacles can be seen dramatically in the image of the *Galaxea* coral on the right.

A second method in the armoury is to extrude mesenterial filaments from the gut, either through the mouth or, more commonly, through a temporary opening in the side wall nearest to the coral to be attacked. These are spread over the neighbouring coral, where they digest its tissue. This is a fast-acting method, taking only a few hours, whereas the production of sweeper tentacles takes several days. However, the sweeper tentacles have been known to reach up to 30 cm (almost 12 in), whereas the mesenterial filaments have a shorter reach of only a few centimetres. Individual corals are able to produce both sweeper tentacles and mesenterial filaments.

A third method, which is used by fast-growing corals, is to tower over slower-growing corals. A tall coral, often of the species *Acropora*, grows upward and outward like an umbrella (called 'overtopping') and shades the coral underneath, thus killing it through lack of sunlight. However, the slower-growing corals are not always

BELOW LEFT: The *Porites* coral in the middle is inhibiting the *Acropora* coral above it from overgrowing and shading it, which would cause the death of the *Porites*.

BELOW CENTRE: The *Halomitra* coral on the bottom is very aggressive and has killed the coral *Lobophyllia* on the top and is overgrowing it.

BELOW RIGHT: The *Halomitra* coral on the left has recently killed the *Montastraea* coral on the right and will grow into the space created.

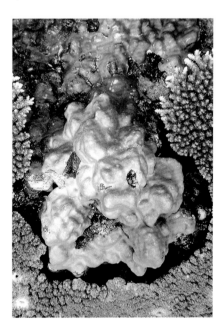

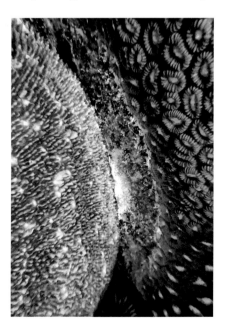

LEFT: The spectacularly long sweeper tentacles from these *Galaxea* specimens, which have been artificially placed together in an aquarium, show just how long a reach some corals can have.

LEFT: For a short range but quick attack the coral can exude mesenterial filaments, as the *Hydnophora* sp shows here. This is less likely to be necessary in the wild but may happen if one coral is knocked onto another. It is unknown if the coral takes any nutrition from the victim.

defenceless and can sometimes inhibit other corals from overtopping them. Finally,
some corals seem to be able to just grow over a neighbouring coral without apparently
having to kill the underlying tissue first. Whatever the method used, the aggressor is
then able to grow over the now dead skeleton of the subordinate coral.

There is a hierarchy of aggressive capability in corals. Some species are able to kill
most others, others are able to kill some but are killed by others, and some at the bottom
of the hierarchy are killed by most others. Yet balance is maintained on the reef because
the less aggressive corals have other strategies to help them, perhaps by growing quickly
as with *Acropora* sp. or by producing many offspring.

Relatives and other reef builders

Closely related to the true, reef-building, corals are the soft corals. They, too, are composed
of polyps in a skeletal matrix, but instead of limestone their skeletons are made mainly
of a gelatinous matrix in which millions of tiny needle-like structures called spicules are
embedded, giving them some rigidity but still allowing them to retain a lot of flexibility.
Whereas the reef-building corals have six, or multiples of six, tentacles and are therefore
called hexacorals, the soft corals have eight tentacles and so are called octocorals. Most

of the soft corals found on a reef also have the photosynthetic zooxanthellae in their tissues, but these species get a greater proportion of their energy needs by capturing plankton from the water, using their stinging cells. Unlike the tentacles of true corals, those of soft corals are feathery, and many are bright and beautiful colours: white, purple, orange, red and yellow, and many shades in between. The greenish-brown colour of the zooxanthellae is not usually dominant in a lot of these species, so the beautiful colours of the soft corals can be seen.

Because many soft corals do not need sunlight for photosynthesis they tend to live at deeper depths on the reef. If we had powerful lighting deep on the reef we would find that life in deeper water is frequently more colourful than it is in the shallows! The soft corals may seem vulnerable to predators, but the spiky spicules embedded in their gelatinous skeletons deter predators, and many soft coral species also contain potent toxins such as terpenes (a group of chemicals that are also found in the resin of some conifers, particularly pine trees). The name 'terpene' is derived from the word 'turpentine', which is a fluid composed of terpenes. The soft corals use these chemicals for defence and to kill adjacent hard corals to make room for their own expansion.

BELOW: The beautiful feathery tentacles of the soft corals are well designed for catching drifting plankton from the water as here at Peros Banhos Atoll in the British Indian Ocean Territory.

RIGHT: The pink crustose coralline algae (CCA) is far more prevalent on a reef than it might seem – unless it is looked for. It is crucial in reef construction and juvenile corals settle on it preferentially.

Another important reef inhabitant that lays down important skeletal material is one that grows everywhere on the reef but often passes unnoticed. This is coralline red algae. Species of this unusual group of plants appear at first glance to be 'bare' reef rock. But closer inspection shows what often looks like a pinkish-red paint coating the spaces between the corals. This is the coralline algae. It is very unusual indeed to find much 'bare' space on a reef; spaces between the larger organisms are filled with small organisms, filling in all around. Often in, around and over these, grows what is referred to as crustose coralline algae (CCA). As the name suggests, these have an encrusting method of growth. The CCA is important because as well as laying down limestone it contributes to the cementation of the reef. It produces a different type of limestone from corals; whereas corals produce aragonite, the CCAs produce calcite.

Coral shapes and budding

One immediately obvious observation when you look at a reef, either as a diver or snorkeller, or even when just looking at photographs, is the huge range of shapes and sizes seen in corals. Close up you can see great variety, caused by widely ranging polyp sizes as well as colony sizes, from tiny single polyp corals to colonies of millions of polyps.

Colony shape plays a large part in where the coral can thrive on the reef. A fragile branching or plate coral has difficulty surviving the pounding breakers in the shallows during a storm, but some sturdy, energy-dispersing dome-shaped corals thrive there. Conversely, dome-shaped corals do not have the best shape to take advantage of the lower light levels at greater depths, where they are outcompeted by large, flat, plate corals, which reach out from the reef in the still waters to catch the low levels of light that penetrate down that far. Branching corals tend to be most common in mid-depths, although sturdy, heavily calcified forms, such as branching *Isopora palifera*, thrive in the pounding surf zone and shallowest areas.

The way a colony is shaped depends partly on how its polyps divide, and they can do this in one of two main ways. Extratentacular budding is when a new, small, daughter polyp buds from the outside of the corallite of the parent polyp and then grows (it is called *extra*tentacular because the daughter appears *outside* the parent's ring of tentacles). The daughter corallite is smaller than the parent and appears squeezed into the small

BELOW LEFT: Coral polyps of the genus *Montastraea* bud extratentacularly, meaning that daughter (smaller) polyps appear outside the parent polyps' ring of tentacles.

BELOW: Coral polyps of the genus *Favia* bud intratentacularly, meaning that daughter (smaller) polyps appear inside the parents' polyps ring of tentacles; the parent polyp 'pinches off' the two daughter polyps.

RIGHT: A skeleton of the coral *Favia pallida* showing intratentacular budding in corallites at various stages of division.

BELOW: A close up of a *Favia pallida* corallite showing the septa. Each corallite is home to a soft-tissued polyp.

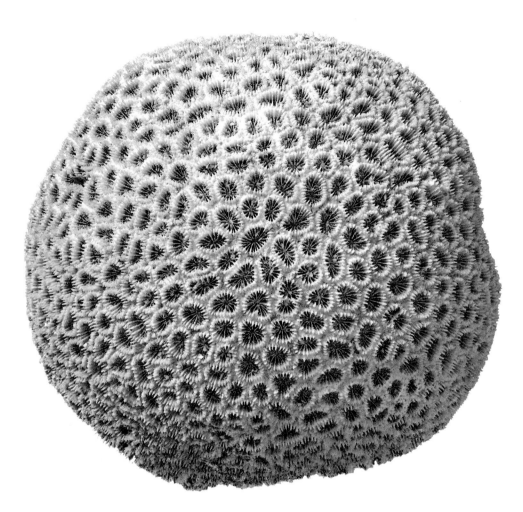

DNA IDENTIFICATION

Coral identification depends very heavily on morphology – the shape of the coral – and this has been the basis of all coral taxonomy (naming and categorizing) so far. An alternative methodology, using the genetic material of an organism to determine the organism's evolutionary history and grouping organisms based on their descent from a common ancestor, is called molecular phylogenetics. Every organism contains DNA and RNA, and this genetic material is passed down from generation to generation. Species that have recently diverged still have a high degree of similarity in their genetic material, and the more dissimilar the species, or the more time that has passed since species separated, the more dissimilar the genetic material is.

This method of using the sequence of genetic material is now widely used to identify the relationships between species, and within and between wider groups such as families. Results from this method are sometimes controversial, suggesting that some species be moved from groupings that they seem to fit into extremely well using morphology, to very different groups. It is currently turning coral taxonomy upside down so that it is in a state of flux, with some coral biologists staying with morphological techniques while others favour the new molecular methods. However combining both approaches gives us better results, as each approach has its own strengths and weaknesses.

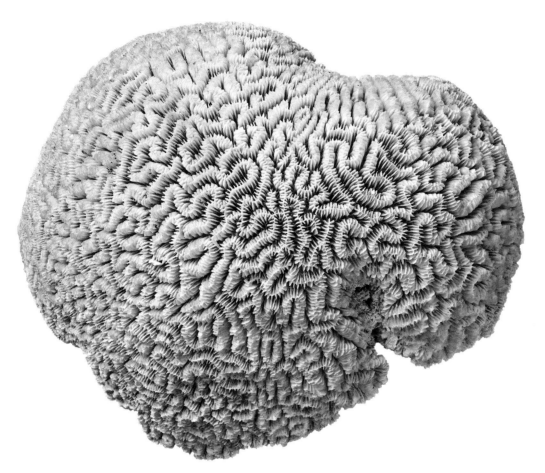

ABOVE: A close-up of the brain coral, *Ctenella chagius,* shows the valleys where the much more connected polyps are found.

LEFT: The skeleton of the brain coral, *Ctenella chagius,* showing the meandering valleys which result when the individual corallites do not pinch off – a long chain of connected polyps, with many mouths inside the ring of tentacles.

available space. As the colony grows upwards and outwards more space becomes available and the new corallite will attain full size. Intratentacular budding is when the polyp constricts around the middle until it is pinched into two daughter polyps. These two polyps then grow upwards and deposit their own limestone corallites around themselves. In intratentacular budding, the size of the daughter corallites varies with different species. In some the division is even, for example in the genus *Favia*, but in the genus *Favites* for example, uneven sized daughter corallites are produced. An important variation of this occurs when intratentacular budding does not complete the pinching-off process but instead the polyp keeps dividing, forming lines of polyps inside a long, communal, meandering corallite that has many mouths opening into a single elongated stomach. These are often referred to as 'brain corals'.

PREVIOUS PAGE: The endangered green turtle, *Chelonia mydas*, is a herbivorous turtle that grazes on seagrass beds. It is highly migratory and travels long distances between feeding grounds and nesting beaches.

Some of the most lively and attractive reef creatures are the reef fish. Colourful and darting, in every shape and size, the great diversity of fish on the reef is often more noticeable than that of any other group of reef dwellers, including the corals themselves. Clouds of fish can be so thick that they obscure the reef, and their coloration can be complex, but always beautiful.

Fish feeding strategies

Fish fill every niche in the sea and show extraordinary adaptations to different habitats. This is no less so on the coral reef, where each species is adapted to survive in its niche. At the top of the food web are the predators, which prey on smaller fish: the fast-swimming shark and barracuda, which chase their prey, and the grouper, which lurks among the corals to ambush unwary fish passing by. Many reef fish feed on the abundant small invertebrates on the reef. These vary from the beautiful angelfish to the schools of goatfish, which sweep across sand patches feeling with their barbels for small prey just under the surface. Even large fish such as the stingray eat small invertebrates in the sand. Other tiny fish are the 'plankton pickers' that daintily pick individual plankton

RIGHT: The saddled butterflyfish, *Chaetodon ephippium*, is a large butterflyfish that is common through the Indo-Pacific region in areas of rich coral growth. It feeds on a large range of items including coral polyps, small invertebrates and sponges.

out of the surrounding water. Crucially important in the maintenance of the reef are the herbivores, which graze the algae so that it cannot overgrow the coral. Some fish species feed on the coral itself. For example, some butterflyfish and the orange spotted filefish, *Oxymonacanthus longirostris*, use their long snouts to pick out and eat polyps individually.

One of the most unusual feeding strategies is that of the cleaner wrasse, which sets up a cleaning station on the reef and attracts other fish by performing a 'dance', which involves swimming head up in a jerking manner. Fish queue to have their parasites removed, and eaten, by this little striped fish. It is a meticulous cleaner, carefully going over every part of its 'client', including inside the mouth of patient and cooperative predators. In a perhaps even stranger feeding strategy, the sabre-toothed blenny mimics the coloration

ABOVE: A cloud of small convict surgeonfish, *Acanthus triostegus*, on Ningaloo Reef, Western Australia. These are an important constituent of the food chain for both larger reef fish and pelagic fish.

ABOVE: The coloration of this grouper on a reef in Ofira, Janub Sina, Egypt makes it easy for it to remain undetected as it lies in wait for unsuspecting prey to swim by.

and behaviour of the cleaner wrasse – but this little blenny, after initial cleaning behaviour, attacks and bites a chunk out of the client fish.

In areas where there is a lot of fishing, fish tend to be cautious and keep their distance, unless they are fed. However, in places where they are unused to people they are unwary and allow divers to come close. Even huge mature grouper will, in a site where people are mostly absent, allow a diver to come very near. Many larger fish school in deeper water near the reef. These are pelagic fish (those that swim in the open sea) and are mostly carnivorous, although manta rays and whale sharks are notable exceptions, as they filter large quantities of seawater to extract their plankton food.

The importance of the grazers

Reef fish, like all other reef inhabitants, have an integral function in maintaining the health of the reef and have a very close relationship with the health of the coral. They are the biggest group of herbivores on a reef, and as such play a very important role in keeping growing algae cropped. As in any healthy habitat, everything is in a delicate balance.

The fish and other herbivores, such as sea urchins and some molluscs, are key in maintaining this balance. Algae are very fast growers and if they get a foothold on a reef they can soon swamp the substrate and make it difficult for slower-growing corals to establish. There are many instances worldwide where the removal of fish through overfishing has seriously damaged a reef. Firstly, the greatly increased biomass of algae that is usually cropped by grazers provides hugely more organic biomass for bacteria and other microbes, and this has been strongly implicated in coral mortality. Secondly, when the grazing herbivores are removed, there is nothing to keep the algae in check, and so the reef corals are likely to become overgrown. The algae prevent corals from settling and shade out ones already there, leading to their death. The coral reef habitat can change to an algae-dominated limestone platform relatively rapidly. With the corals gone, those organisms that depend on them can no longer survive, and the biodiversity of the area becomes impoverished. When corals are replaced by algae, this is termed a phase-shift, and once it happens it is very hard to reverse. The new state may be a very stable ecological condition.

Other important herbivores are sea urchins, which graze by scraping at the coral rock. Their removal has had spectacularly deleterious consequences in the Caribbean. There, disease virtually wiped out the grazing urchin, *Diadema,* in 1983–84; it is thought that the disease was caused by a new pathogen entering the Caribbean via the Panama Canal. These urchins had taken on an increased importance in terms of grazing, as a large proportion of the Caribbean's grazing fish had already been caught by that date. There was no effective 'redundancy' from different grazers any longer, and so reef ecosystems as a whole lost their resilience in terms of keeping algae in check. The result has been a massive decline in coral cover and increase in algae throughout the Caribbean.

There is, and needs to be, a certain amount of resilience in a healthy coral reef, but unfortunately, removal of a stressor does not automatically allow the reef to recover to its previous state. If stress is applied, whether it is overfishing or some other form of exploitation, it may appear for a while not to be causing any harm. However, after a certain point the reef deteriorates rapidly and declines to a phase-shifted state. At that point, even if the fishing was stopped for example, recovery might not take place because the new phase-shifted state is very stable.

BELOW LEFT: The energetics of a phase-shift. The valleys represent different ecological states: coral-dominated on the left, algae-dominated on the right. Top: the 'coral valley' is stable and healthy, and the black ball settles in the valley. If it is pushed too hard, or if the separating 'hill' is eroded by an external force such as pollution, it is pushed into the lower valley. Once it is in the lower valley or shifted phase it remains there until some other force changes it – it will not readily move back up to the 'coral valley'.

BELOW: This used to be a beautiful, healthy reef in Mahé in the Seychelles, but due to fishing and local pollution, the reef has not recovered from the ocean surface layer warming that occurred throughout the Indian Ocean in 1998. It is now predominantly an algal seabed.

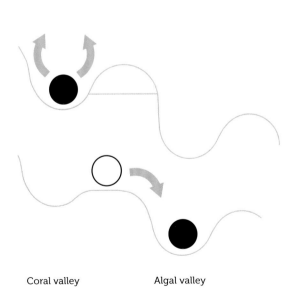

Coral valley   Algal valley

Molluscs, sponges and crustaceans

Competing with the reef fish in the attractiveness stakes are the gastropod molluscs, or snails, with their beautifully shaped and coloured shells. Most are usually very cryptic organisms, meaning that they remain hidden – under corals, ledges of rock, or concealed among the seaweeds. They feed on a large array of prey, with some species of cone shell even able to catch fish, which they do with a long poison-tipped dart whose swift acting toxin can also be fatal to humans. These predatory molluscs mostly lie hidden in sand and harpoon small fish as they swim past. But most molluscs feed the way land snails do, using a long ribbon of tiny hooked teeth called a radula, which they use to scrape up algae. Some use the radula not as a scraper but as a drill to bore through the shells of other molluscs; they then pour digestive juices through the hole and suck out the pre-digested 'soup'. A few molluscs feed on corals; here there is no need to bore through the skeleton because the polyp tissue is on the top – the mollusc just sits on the coral and sucks! One of these corallivorous molluscs, a species of *Drupella*, can sometimes reach plague proportions and kill large swathes of coral.

RIGHT: Molluscs are generally fairly cryptic on the reef, usually hidden and hard to see, like this penguin wing oyster, *Pteria penguin*, in Koh Tao, Thailand.

Sponges make up another large group on the reef. These, like the corals and soft corals, are sessile and remain attached to the substrate. Sponges are filter feeders, filtering bacteria and plankton from the seawater, so these play a major role in the health of the reef. They take in water through an inhalant pore and, after filtering out food and oxygen, expel the water out of an exhalent pore. Some sponges bore into limestone, including coral skeletons and mollusc shells. They secrete a chemical that kills the coral polyps before boring into the limestone skeletons using different chemicals. Significant areas of reef can be weakened and eroded away by large sheets of these boring sponges. Many sponges have symbiotic inhabitants just as the corals do – in this case bacteria instead of zooxanthellae.

The crustaceans – crabs and lobsters and their relatives – are another colourful reef-dwelling group. These range from the large reef lobster, living in almost every accessible cook and cranny in the reef to tiny, exquisitely coloured crabs, which live among the coral branches. Small shrimp are common throughout the reef, including specialists such as cleaner shrimp, which assiduously clean parasites from creatures that come near them. Each of these groups of organisms can fill an entire book by themselves, and here we can touch on only a few of them.

LEFT: Large, colourful, sponges on reefs at Poor Knights Islands Marine Reserve, New Zealand, where they play the important role of filtering plankton from the water, which keeps the water clear and allows more sunlight to reach the corals.

BELOW: This encrusting sponge sheet is in the process of enveloping the coral, which will eventually be killed and overgrown.

RIGHT: Like the cleaner
fish, the Caribbean spotted
cleaner shrimp, *Periclimenes
yucatanicus*, performs the
valuable role of removing
parasites from other reef
creatures, and because of this it
is safe from predation.

RIGHT: Crustaceans, like this
species of hermit crab, remain
hidden in crevices on the reef
and form part of the diet of many
other species, such as larger fish
and octopuses.

Reef plankton

All reef inhabitants are important, but some have more obvious roles than others. It might be argued that the corals are the most important members of the reef community, as they build the reef upon which everything else is dependent. But perhaps another group might wear that crown – a group upon which even the corals are dependent: the plankton. 'Plankton' is a name given not to a taxonomic group of specific creatures but rather a collection of all manner of small organisms that drift with the ocean currents. There are both plant plankton (called phytoplankton) and animal plankton (called zooplankton). Each comprises a wide range of different organisms, from the larvae of many marine creatures to a large group of small organisms of different taxonomic groups including bacteria, copepods and some jellyfish. Plankton are the basis of many of the reef's food chains for all but the herbivores, as they are filtered out of the water by many organisms that are then eaten themselves by those further up the chain.

Plankton are rarely distributed evenly throughout the water column and although the phytoplankton stay near the surface to photosynthesize, most zooplankton have a diurnal (daily) vertical migration. They spend daylight hours in crevices in the reef and among the grains of sand and rubble and spend the night in the surface waters above the reef. Why they do this is not completely known, but it is probably either to avoid predators that hunt visually or to avoid higher water temperatures that would make them metabolize faster. They start to rise in enormous numbers before dusk to spend the night in the shallow waters and before dawn they sink again. Although they may avoid many other predators with this behaviour, it means that they pass the reef when the corals have their polyps extended to feed, which benefits the corals greatly.

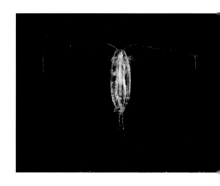

ABOVE: Copepods are small crustaceans, one of the dominant components of zooplankton and a major food source for many of the larger marine organisms such as fish, whales and seabirds. Different species are found throughout the world's oceans where they are perhaps a larger contributor to oceanic secondary production than all other organisms together.

Important nearby habitats

Coral reefs usually do not exist in isolation. Just as the life on a reef is interlocking, so reefs have connections with other habitats. These important adjuncts to many coral reefs include mangroves and seagrass beds. Whereas most plants on the reef are algae, the mangroves and seagrasses are angiosperms, like land plants. Mangroves, with their frequently muddy waters, may seem to be an entirely unrelated habitat to coral reefs, but an important link exists between the two. Mangroves are salt-tolerant trees that form forests in coastal regions and, where they grow near coral reefs, have

ABOVE: Although mangroves are land plants, they are also important to reefs in many ways, from fish and crustacean nurseries to sediment traps. They also help to protect the coast from erosion.

a crucial, close relationship with the reef. They are important nutrient-rich nursery grounds for many reef fish and other reef organisms such as shrimp. These breeding grounds are vital for commercially valuable species too, and so are important for local economies. Juveniles of many species spend their early stages in the relatively safe environment of the tangle of mangrove roots, which are impenetrable to large predators. When they are larger, and therefore have more refuge in size, they move out to the reef, where they live their adult life.

The mangroves also play an important part in stabilizing and trapping sediment coming from the land that might otherwise damage the reef. Their roots slow the water flow. The reef in return acts as a breakwater, providing the calm waters that the mangroves prefer. Nutrients in run-off from the land are also filtered and retained by the mangroves; mangroves need nutrients but the external addition of nutrients is very damaging to coral reefs. Toxins and pollutants become bound to and trapped among the small particles, which are then deposited in the sediment.

Along with the coral reefs, mangroves are also an extra line of defence against natural destructive events such as cyclones and tsunamis. After the hugely destructive typhoon Haiyan in the Philippines in November 2013, and the Banda Aceh tsunami in December 2004, areas that were protected by mangrove forests received less damage than areas where the mangroves had been removed. The mangroves also prevent erosion following events like these. Destruction of mangroves by people is unfortunately severe because mangroves are often seen as unproductive land and so are often cleared for agriculture or shrimp farming. The wood is also used for firewood. There are now several mangrove-replanting campaigns throughout the tropics.

BELOW: For reef fish and other organisms such as some crustaceans, the link between mangroves and coral reefs is critical. Removal or damage to one of the habitats affects the other.

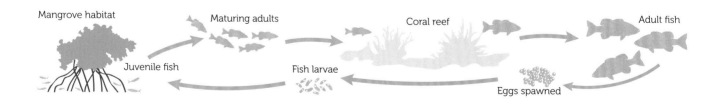

Mangrove habitat   Maturing adults   Coral reef   Adult fish
              Juvenile fish   Fish larvae   Eggs spawned

Seagrasses are usually found growing in extensive meadows. They are important in two main respects: they supply food for several of the reef's inhabitants, such as schools of fish that migrate between reef and seagrass beds, as well as those most iconic inhabitants, green turtles and dugong. Some of the fish that raise their young in mangroves or coral reefs spend much of their lives among the seagrass. Like the mangroves, the seagrass beds trap sediment and nutrients, which benefits them and the adjacent coral reefs. It used to be thought that very few reef organisms graze directly on the huge seagrass beds because of their poor nutritional content, but new research has revealed that more species do and that they are a very important link in the food chain, with several birds using them as significant feeding grounds too. Most of the food transfer occurs through microbial action, however. When the seagrass dies, microbes decompose them and the material and energy that the seagrasses have accumulated from the sun goes into the reef's food web.

ABOVE: Where seagrass occurs it often forms extensive beds such as here at Great Chagos Bank, British Indian Ocean Territory. These are important feeding grounds for marine creatures such as dugong and green turtles.

For both mangroves and seagrasses, recycling of dead material requires microbial action. Microbes are an invisible yet key group on the reef. As on land, there are beneficial microbes and harmful ones. The beneficial ones break down dead organisms and return the nutrients into the system, and so are an essential part of the food web. It has also been suggested that some of these beneficial microbes have a close association with corals and can fix nitrogen, which is then passed on to the zooxanthellae, benefiting both the coral and the zooxanthellae in this way too.

Microbes are everywhere. It has been estimated that there are about 100 million microbes and an astonishing one trillion viruses on each square centimetre of healthy coral tissue. A single healthy coral can have almost 30,000 different species of microbe on its surface. In a healthy reef these do no harm, but in certain circumstances, such as where there is pollution, they may become harmful and cause disease in corals and in many different reef inhabitants. With warming seas and coastal pollution of tropical waters, this is proposed as the main reason for the death of many of the corals in the Caribbean region(see page 46).

TIME

A coral reef is a biological structure built by organisms in the sea that lay down a solid mineral foundation. They become built up when those organisms grow upward and outwards from the base laid down by previous generations. The resulting structure is the reef, home to a rich and diverse community of organisms. The rock it is made of is calcium carbonate, commonly known as limestone, which has many related crystalline forms. As already noted, corals lay down this carbonate in a crystalline form known as aragonite, but another crystalline form of carbonate laid down by many other marine organisms is calcite.

The coral polyps extract the materials to make their limestone homes from the seawater, and this limestone builds up the coral skeletons, firstly, and these then make up the bulk of the reef. Alongside this growth is erosion. The reef is full of organisms that bore into the limestone of the reef for refuge or for food and in doing so produce rubble, sand and silt – even this contributes to the growth of the reef, because some of the rubble, sand and silt is consolidated in a process that cements the reef, rather like the mortar that holds the brickwork of a wall together. This cementation process makes the reef stronger and more durable. The skeletons of other organisms, such as the siliceous (silica-containing) spicules of sponges, and the aragonite and calcite remains of soft corals, molluscs, crustaceans, calcareous algae and plankton, and numerous other creatures, all contribute to the reef-building process, too.

Past reef builders

All corals today belong to the same taxonomic group, the order Scleractinia. Fossil records show that these corals first appeared in Triassic seas about 240 million years ago, and they have been the main reef builders ever since. In addition to scleractinian corals, there have been many other biological reefs throughout the world, but they were built by some very different creatures.

Starting in Precambrian times, the very first group of primitive organisms to build reefs were microbes such as cyanobacteria, which grew as thin mats but trapped sediments and built up structures from the sea floor. For example, stromatolites were cabbage-shaped masses of sediment bound together by microbial sheets; other structures in microbial reefs included thrombolites, which grew as pillar-shaped masses with a clotted-cream-like texture. The fossilized remains of these structures are evidence of some of the most ancient life on Earth: fossils of the earliest microbialites are more than 3.5 billion years

PREVIOUS PAGE: Aerial view of Kri Island, Raja Ampat, West Papua, Indonesia.

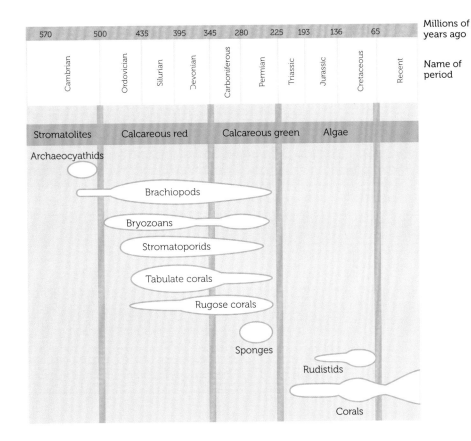

LEFT: A timeline showing the periods in which the different reef builders dominated the oceans and when they became extinct.

BELOW: A small block of limestone, 5 cm (2 in) across, from the Cambrian rocks of South Australia, containing sectioned specimens of the archaeocyathan sponge, *Metaldetes*.

old. They are thought to be important organisms that, early on in the primeval Earth, were responsible for producing the oxygen that led to the oxygen-rich atmosphere we have today. Stromatolites still exist today, growing mainly in hypersaline (very salty) habitats, the most famous of which are in Shark Bay in Western Australia, where the habitat is too hot and too saline for grazers to live.

With the first appearance of skeletonized marine invertebrates in the Cambrian, new reef builders entered the picture and lived alongside the stromatolite microbial communities. Most important during this time are various groups of sponges, in particular the small vase-shaped archaeocyathids, which were able provide sufficient carbonate to build up reefs but became extinct by the Middle Cambrian (around 520 million years ago). Other groups of extinct sponges also contributed significantly to reef building since the Cambrian, including the chatetids and the stromatoporoids, which are related to modern-day sclerosponges.

RIGHT: Even though stromatolites are some of the earliest forms of life on Earth, they are still in existence today, most famously in Western Australia.

BELOW: A section through a fossil stromatolite originating from the Precambrian rocks of Eastern Siberia 2,500-2,000 million years old; specimen size, 23 cm (9 in) left to right.

Earliest corals

Two groups of coral first appeared at this time too: Tabulata and Rugosa. Although they are cnidarians like modern corals, they are distinct groups. The tabulate corals were colonial and had hexagonal corallites 1–3 mm (a tiny fraction of an inch) in diameter. They laid down a calcite skeleton to form substantial reefs. Although it is not known for certain, it is possible that these tabulate corals also had symbiotic zooxanthellae. The early rugose corals were commonly simple, solitary corals, characterized by four-fold symmetry – compared with modern reef corals, which have six-fold symmetry, and soft corals, which have eight-fold symmetry. Many were horn-shaped, and some could grow

to almost a metre (3 ft) in length. Later, more complex colonial forms evolved that can look superficially like modern-day corals.

Between the Permian period and the Triassic, about 252 million years ago, there occurred the Earth's greatest extinction event. This great extinction was probably a result of large amounts of carbon dioxide being released into the atmosphere, which caused the planet to warm rapidly because of a strong 'greenhouse' effect. This was known as the Permo–Triassic (P–T) extinction, when a large proportion of the world's species – estimated to be about 96% of marine species – became extinct. Both tabulate and rugose corals and the stromatoporoids disappeared during the P–T extinction event, and the numbers of reef-building brachiopods and bryozoans were severely diminished.

With the removal of so much reef diversity, microbial communities again became the dominant reef builders for a few tens of million years following the P–T event. In a way, the extinction event set the biosphere back to Cambrian conditions, allowing new groups of organisms to colonize and adapt to shallow habitats in the sea and begin to form reefs.

In the middle of the Triassic period the modern-day scleractinian corals first appeared and started to lay down reef structures. (The so-called 'naked coral' hypothesis posits that non-skeletonized, soft-bodied ancestors of the scleractinians, similar to sea anemones, had been living on Earth for hundreds of millions of years but only appear as fossils once they had evolved the ability to secrete a limestone skeleton that was preserved in the rocks.) Their fortunes waxed and waned too, and their diversity and abundance declined in response to past global and regional environmental changes, but they never disappeared and always recovered, to become the main reef-building creatures that we see today. Another group of reef builders appeared alongside them for a while, the Rudistids, a group of giant clams. Like most others, these became extinct, but during their period of flourishing in the Jurassic and Cretaceous periods they built large reef-like structures in association with corals. Just as with today's reefs, all these ancient reefs supported a diverse group of organisms.

BELOW: The solitary fossil rugose coral, *Streptelasma,* from the Ordovician rocks of the USA (484–442 million years ago), measuring almost 4 cm (1½ in) in length.

BELOW RIGHT: A small colony, 4 cm (1½ in) wide, of the fossil tabulate coral *Heliolites* from Silurian rocks in England (442–422 million years ago).

LEFT: The Wren's Nest site in the West Midlands, England is a Site of Special Scientific Interest (SSSI) and one of the most important geological locations in Britain. It is famous for its diverse and rich coral reef fossils from the Silurian period 428 million years ago.

Many of these ancient reefs became fossilized and are visible today in many parts of the world. Scientists study the diversity and habitats in these preserved reefs to learn how they responded to ancient episodes of environmental change, in order to better understand how modern reefs are likely to respond to present-day changes. Some fossil reefs are now thousands of metres up mountains and many are well inland, indicating the locations of the ancient seas in which they were laid down. They are found in many places around the world; New Mexico, USA has a very complete fossil record, the island of Gotland in Sweden, Sichuan Province in central China and the Canadian Rockies are also very rich in fossil coral reefs. There are several places in Britain also, the Wren's Nest site near Dudley in the West Midlands being a well-known example. Some of these fossil reefs, through complex geology, have been metamorphosed into attractive varieties of limestone. One beautiful example of these, the black Ashburton Limestone, can be seen covering the walls inside the entrance to the Natural History Museum in London, where the polished surfaces show intricate sponge and coral fossils.

BELOW: At the Wren's Nest site there is also a fossil ripple bed. Ancient Silurian storms caused deep ripples in the soft substrate that were preserved when they were covered in mud, and all of this became rock over time, including the ripples.

Modern reef structures

Several kinds of modern reef structure are recognized today, yet they are all formed in a common process. Corals grow up towards the sunlight but, being marine creatures, must stay below the surface of the water. When they cannot grow up any more, they grow out laterally. If they grow out too far, the expanding reef edge becomes too steep and overhangs, causing it to topple down the face of the reef, just as an overhanging cliff can. Adjacent deep water limits how far out from the shore that reef can grow.

Some coral reefs grow along the shoreline of a coast: they fringe the coast and are therefore called fringing reefs. The largest fringing reef in the world is the Ningaloo Reef off Western Australia. When the coastline retreats inland, perhaps as a result of rising sea levels, the fringing reef, which is able to grow and keep up with the rising sea level, is left offshore. At this point it is called a barrier reef. The distinction between a fringing reef and a barrier reef is usually when the channel between the shore and the reef becomes navigable by shipping. The biggest and best-known example of a barrier reef is the Great Barrier Reef along the east coast of Australia.

RIGHT: Waves breaking on one of the thousands of shallow reefs off Bermuda. Corals are constantly growing and being eroded, and the effect of this is that the reef is maintained.

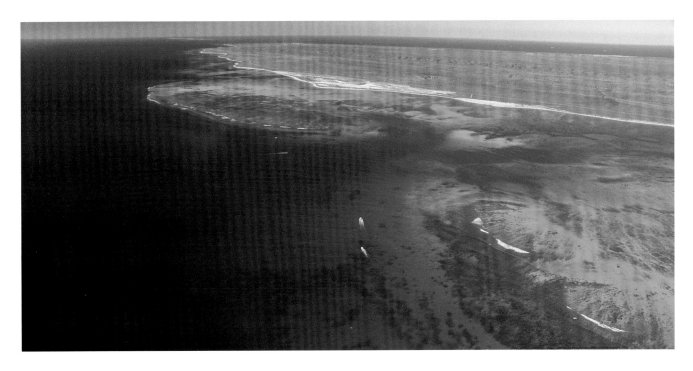

ABOVE: The Ningaloo Reef is the longest fringing reef in the world. It is also famous for the annual migration of whale sharks and humpback whales, which pass close by.

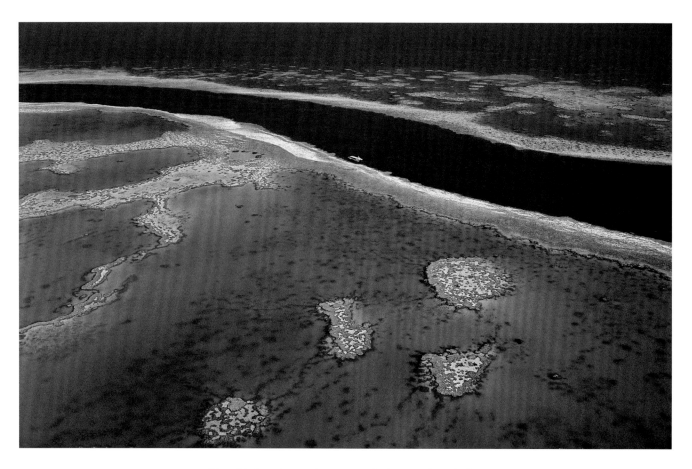

ABOVE: The Great Barrier Reef off the eastern coast of Australia is the biggest barrier reef in the world. It is very rich in marine life, but like many other reefs is threatened by development.

The third major reef structure is the coral atoll. Charles Darwin was the scientist who worked out how atolls develop, and his work illustrates the coming together of biology and geology. The first stage in the creation of an atoll is a tropical volcanic island, around which a fringing reef grows. Volcanoes subside over time. As the volcanic island subsides, the fringing reef becomes a barrier reef. The island continues to subside until it becomes completely submerged, leaving only the ring of reef, which has continued to grow upwards to the water surface. This ring of reefs is the atoll. This sequence of events, from barrier reef to atoll, takes millions of years. It has subsequently been shown that Darwin was correct in his theory, as very deep cores have been taken through some atolls which show that, after varying depths of limestone, volcanic rock lies below, sometimes several kilometres deep.

These are the three classical reef structures. Given the complexities of shorelines and of land movements over geological time, several more have been found and named

LEFT: The Maldives consist of a series of coral atolls formed when that part of the continental crust was over a volcanic hotspot 55 million years ago.

BELOW: Diagram showing the classic Darwinian atoll formation theory. It took many years to conclusively prove that Darwin was correct, when drilling encountered volcanic rock deep below a thick cap of reef limestone.

that do not quite conform to these categorizations. Important ones are patch reefs, in which the corals grow in shallow areas and produce a maze of small reefs and channels. Basically, wherever conditions are right for corals in terms of suitable shallow depths and clear and warm water, reefs develop.

The series of ice ages that have occurred in the past few million years have left their mark on coral reefs, too. When much of the world's seawater was taken up into the vast ice caps and glaciers 20,000 years ago, the global sea level was reduced

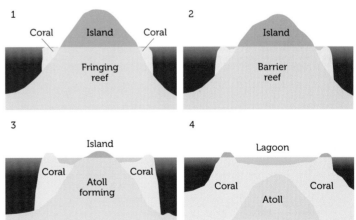

by as much as 180 m (590 ft). Underwater on many coral reefs there are wave-cut platforms and caves indicating where the sea level was for prolonged periods of time. The exposed corals would all have died, having been left high and dry, but species that managed to retreat downwards with the receding surface repopulated the reefs as the

water rose again. To complicate things further, sometimes sea level was a lot higher than it is today, such as during warm periods in the Earth's history before the ice caps had developed. Then reefs developed at those higher elevations. Added to that, many of those ancient reefs have been pushed up as mountains formed, leaving many fossil reefs at altitudes of hundreds or even thousands of metres. These fossil reefs can be seen in mountain ranges in many places round the world.

Modern research

Coral reef scientists use a huge array of techniques to understand reefs, including scuba equipment to study reefs directly and satellite mapping to chart them accurately. These, and other technologies mean that great advances have been made in our understanding of these habitats in the past 60 years or so. Before the advent of scuba, reef research was either confined to the reef flat or to very shallow areas using glass-bottomed buckets or boxes. Deeper areas were surveyed using lines with a weight covered in sticky black pitch at the end, in the hope that something interesting would adhere to it. As much of the life on the reef is attached to the substrate, this would not have produced a very clear picture of what was down there and often the only bits retrieved like this were dead and broken fragments. Since scientists have been able to go to look, measure and set up instruments, perhaps the most important discovery that has been made about reefs is their huge biodiversity. A healthy reef is the most biodiverse system on Earth, teeming with life.

Much reef research to this day is devoted to trying to understand the ways that all of this biodiversity works together and to better understand how reefs work. Coral reefs are hugely important to people, for providing food, for shoreline protection and the provision of biodiversity. Added to that, a large amount of the scientific research now relates to the problems caused by their overexploitation and to the damaging effects of global climate change caused by humans releasing too much carbon dioxide into the atmosphere. There has been speculation by some scientists that the warming and ocean acidification that is happening as a result of this may lead to another large extinction event for coral reefs. This huge problem for reefs is discussed in detail on pages 82–95.

BELOW: Scientists use many survey methods in their coral reef research, some as simple as observing and recording on slates as shown here during a coral bleaching event in Kaneohe Bay, Hawaii

TO PEOPLE

PREVIOUS PAGE: A healthy thriving reef, like this one near Batangas in the Philippines, can support a local community, so it is in their economic interest to maintain the reef in good condition.

BELOW: Often small, and always very low lying, coral islands are vulnerable to both natural hazards, such as hurricanes, and to human-made threats, such as climate change.

The benefits that we gain from natural ecosystems such as rainforests, grasslands, tundra and coral reefs are known as 'ecosystem services'. There has been an increasing awareness of the huge value to people of ecosystem services in the last couple of decades as a result of the work of scientists, economists and politicians who have produced a series of reports evaluating the condition of the world's ecosystems and the varied services that they provide. In monetary terms they found that the value of the intact ecosystems exceeds substantially the amount of the global gross domestic product, or GDP. Alarmingly, the ability of ecosystems to provide the services that we rely on are being compromised by many human-related environmental impacts. The World Resources Institute's *Reefs at Risk Revisited,* 2011 report, along with several others, are similar assessments that look purely at coral reefs. More broad-ranging ones, including

the United Nations' *Millennium Ecosystem Assessment,* published between 2001 and 2005, all found similar results showing that the value of ecosystems decreased markedly when they were damaged.

It has very recently been estimated that coral reefs now provide a global value of about US$9 trillion per year. These benefits include obvious direct ones such as fishing, pharmaceutical chemicals and tourism. But there are other less obvious indirect benefits, such as providing shoreline protection – which is becoming increasingly important to coastal communities – the provision of nursery habitats for commercial species, and the scientific value and cultural value of the reefs.

One important – you might say the most important – benefit is that some small islands on coral reefs are entirely dependent on them for their existence. Many of the world's coral islands owe their entire existence to the corals that built them up in the first place, and which now continue to maintain them above sea level. Low-lying atolls such as the Maldives and many of the vast number of small coral islands in the Pacific and Indian oceans fall into this category, including the islands of the Chagos Archipelago, which are given as a case study on page 102. This service becomes even more important as sea levels are expected to rise in the coming centuries. These islands are closely linked to the coral reef and are in fact an extension of the reef itself, an integral part of it.

We should perhaps not become entirely caught up in the monetary value of coral reefs, although that is often what is needed to convince governments to protect them. Local people also derive food from them, and tourists from around the world derive huge enjoyment and pleasure from the beauty and splendour of the reef. This is worth an incalculable amount.

Reef fisheries

The area of coral reef that is fished is only 0.1% of the ocean, yet it produces between 2 and 5% of fisheries production. Most coral reefs are located alongside the poorest and most highly populated nations, where they provide an essential food source for a large number of people, particularly those living in small isolated locations. Much of the coral reef fishery is subsistence fishing, directly used to feed the local people, but there is an increasing trend in the live fish trade for the fish not to be consumed by local people but exported as a 'cash crop' to developed nations, thus providing significant income for local fishers. Tropical marine aquaria too have become very popular in the past couple of

decades, primarily in countries far from coral reefs. Fish are caught alive and transported via a series of dealers to Western markets, where they can sell for very high prices. So a healthy coral reef provides both subsistence and commercial fisheries. A healthy population of fish on a local reef is excellent food security for local people, which is obviously something to be greatly desired.

Reefs supply more than fin fish to the coastal communities. Catching octopuses such as *Octopus cyanea* is a very important subsistence and economic activity, especially in the western Indian Ocean. The octopuses are gleaned from reef flats and by snorkelling on the shallow reef, traditionally by women and children. Fishing for another mollusc, the giant clam, *Tridacna gigas,* is a highly profitable fishery in the Maldives, Southeast Asia and the Pacific Islands. It is collected for the meat of the adductor muscle and also for the shell. On Caribbean reefs fishing for the queen conch, *Strombus gigas,* is a traditional fishery, again for the meat of the large muscle and for the shell, which is sold to tourists. Lobsters, crabs and shrimp are all valuable resources, too. The spiny lobster is the main fishery in 24 Caribbean countries and is one of their main sources of overseas income. These and many other reef resources provide valuable incomes for local peoples – pearls, black coral, several molluscs, and sea cucumbers for 'traditional medicine', as well as food and fish for the aquarium trade, all are used in different parts of the world.

LEFT: An artisanal fishery such as the octopus fishery in the western Indian Ocean is critical to local people. When international markets buy the catches it places greater pressure on an already exploited resource.

BELOW LEFT: The queen conch, *Strombus gigas*, fishery is managed in many parts of the Caribbean and is exploited unsustainably in others. Removal of queen conch is prohibited in US waters.

BELOW: The Caribbean spiny lobster, *Panulinus argus*, is a valuable fishery resource that is declining throughout its range. Its loss will threaten local economies.

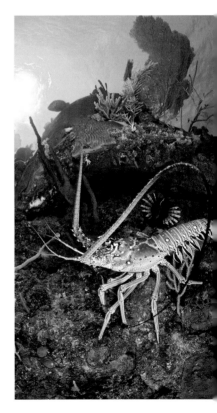

ABOVE: The giant clam, *Tridacna gigas,* is very vulnerable to overcollecting, as it is easy to find and collect. Like corals, it has symbiotic zooxanthellae in its tissues.

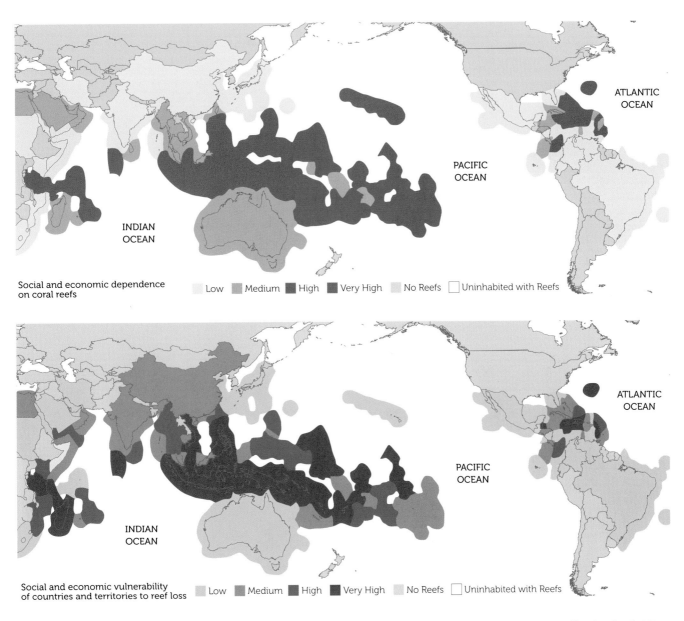

Social and economic dependence
on coral reefs   ▢ Low ▢ Medium ▢ High ▢ Very High ▢ No Reefs ▢ Uninhabited with Reefs

Social and economic vulnerability
of countries and territories to reef loss   ▢ Low ▢ Medium ▢ High ▢ Very High ▢ No Reefs ▢ Uninhabited with Reefs

TOP: Map showing that the countries which have the highest social and economic dependence on reefs are the small coral island states built on coral atolls.

BOTTOM: Map showing that the countries which are socially and economically most vulnerable to reef loss are those with high populations. This means that a very large number of people will be affected by reef decline.

Shoreline protection

From the shoreline of a tropical beach, as you look out towards the edge of the reef, you may see a line of white breakers against the rich blue of the sea. This line of breakers marks the place of one of the most valuable services that coral reefs provide for coastal communities. If it were not for the reefs, the energy of the impacting waves would be expended on the shore itself and erode it away. The edge of the reef (the reef crest) prevents this from happening and is responsible for the maintenance of countless coral islands and shores around the world.

On particularly high-energy shores, there is an algal ridge marking the edge of the reef. This is a natural buttress created by the growth of coralline algae such as *Porolithon*, which is very strong and resistant to the pounding of the surf. As much as 75–95% of the waves' energy is reduced by the ridge and reef together, and if the reefs die they quickly erode and the huge wave energy is spent instead on the newly vulnerable shoreline. In 1998 the El Niño seawater warming killed corals, particularly in the Indian Ocean. This increased the wave energy reaching the shore, leading to the erosion of roads and buildings and resulting in a cost of millions of dollars for shoreline hardening and reinforcement of roads and infrastructure. Reefs also protect inshore habitats such as mangroves, which are valuable nursery grounds for many species of fish and shrimp.

Tourism

Almost 100 countries profit from coral reef tourism, and for many of them this contributes up to 15% of the GDP, and in extreme cases up to 80% of foreign earnings too. The value comes either directly in the form of scuba diving or snorkelling and reef fishing, or by those who just want to enjoy the beautiful coralline beaches.

Coral reefs are widely associated with beautiful white sand beaches. It may be no surprise to learn that this sand comes from ground-down coral eroded from the reef framework by various marine organisms such as sponges, molluscs and particularly parrotfish, as well as from the skeletons of other marine life. There is a dynamic relationship between growth of corals and the building of new reef material, with the breakdown of their coral skeletons and the production of sand. Sand fills in the spaces on the reef and contributes to the growth of the reef, and some helps coral islands to grow. These beautiful sand beaches are valuable assets for tourism. Hotels are built on shores for their clients to enjoy and the income to both developing nations and developed nations – for example Florida in the USA – is significant.

LEFT: The pink coloration of the algal ridge is very distinctive. The hard red coralline algae forms an important protective barrier for shorelines.

BELOW: Where the shore is no longer protected by the reef, erosion becomes a problem for coastal infrastructure, with sand being washed away from some areas and deposited on others. Overall, however, erosion will occur.

RIGHT: Diving tourism is an
important source of revenue for
many tropical countries. As the
best diving is usually in less-
inhabited areas, it is important
income for remote communities.

Scuba diving brings considerable income for many developing countries, usually in the form of much-needed hard currency. Local economies with dive shops, guides, hotels and restaurants all benefit from this tourism. Many countries and tropical islands such as the Maldives and the Caribbean rely heavily on diving tourism – for example, on the Caribbean island of Bonaire over half the tourists in 2007 were divers. The global income from diving tourism is around US$10 billion per year.

The presence of large and iconic reef species brings in large numbers of tourists. At around a dozen locations around the world the seasonal presence of whale sharks contributes significantly to the local economy. Manta ray and shark diving are also popular reef-based tourist attractions. It has often been estimated that a shark, manta ray or large grouper is worth a hundred times more alive as a living attraction than it is dead on a plate – and the value from tourism can be gained year after year, for the life of the animal.

ICONIC SPECIES AND ECOTOURISM

Whale sharks are rarely seen, except at a few reef locations that have abundant plankton for these huge fish to feed on. Because of the restricted number of places where they can easily and reliably be seen, and because of their dramatic size, beauty and gentle nature, and because it is safe for children to swim with them, these places are very popular tourist destinations. The overall loss of potential income caused by hunting whale sharks is enormous.

Most species of shark are in severe decline globally. It is estimated that they are being killed at the rate of about 100 million every year, and the remaining population is estimated to be only 10% of that a few decades ago. Huge numbers are killed for their fins for shark fin soup, mainly for the Chinese market and many more die as careless by-catch.

The manta ray is another iconic reef dweller that, like the whale shark, is large, dramatic and safe to swim with. This majestic creature is hunted for its gill rakers for the Chinese traditional medicine market. In 2014, Indonesia, where mantas were hunted until recently, became the world's biggest sanctuary for mantas, having been persuaded by the fact that a manta ray is worth about US$1 million over its lifetime for tourists to swim with and only US$40 to US$500 dead.

Because many iconic species are now restricted to less-populated reef areas, the ecotourism benefits are even greater, as they provide much-needed income for remote communities. Large turtles, the greens and leatherbacks, are also a popular tourist draw. Another advantage of ecotourism is that it encourages local communities to protect these species when they are increasingly seen as being valuable to them.

Humpback whales are not reef species but can be seen at a few main reef sites – Hawai'i, the Dominican Republic, the Great Barrier Reef and, one of the best, Ningaloo Reef in Western Australia – as they migrate from cold waters to warm tropical waters for the calves to be born. Humpback whales have been protected since 1966, and their population is slowly increasing. Most humpback whale watching is done from boats rather than swimming with them, as they travel so fast and also because of the ethical considerations of swimming with wild mammals that have newly born calves with them.

ABOVE: Swimming with large marine creatures is an exhilarating experience. It requires stringent controls to make sure that the creatures, like this magnificent manta, are not disturbed.

RIGHT: Charismatic species, such as the whale shark, are worth very much more alive than dead, in a financial sense as well as an ecological one.

Pharmaceuticals

Bioprospecting is the name given to the search for new compounds that may have some medicinal benefit. Because of the extraordinary biodiversity on a coral reef, it is a good potential source of new bioactive compounds. Many of the animals on a coral reef use chemicals for defence, aggression and to allow them to make best use of resources on the reef such as light. Painkillers extracted from neurotoxins in cone shells are already in use and are presently being investigated for their potential to produce even more powerful new painkillers, with one species, *Conus magus*, showing promise

to provide a non-addictive extremely powerful painkiller. Other compounds are being investigated that may be used to treat Alzheimer's and Parkinson's diseases. Antiviral and anticancer agents extracted from sponges are already in use, along with many other compounds. A variety of other possibilities, from potential antibiotics to sunscreens, is being investigated as part of a global move towards investigating what human benefits can be gained from what reef animals and plants have been doing for millennia.

ABOVE: *Conus purpurascens* (above) and *Conus textile* (below) are two of the species of cone shell which show great promise in providing powerful new pharmaceuticals. Both species are extremely toxic and very dangerous to humans.

Biodiversity

The loss of biodiversity from around the globe is an increasing problem, and coral reefs are not immune to this. As we have seen, they are the most biodiverse habitats on the planet at higher taxonomic levels, and this biodiversity is one of the huge benefits that coral reefs give to us. Maintenance of biodiversity is of incalculable benefit in preserving healthy and functioning ecosystems. Although this is a resource that is difficult to quantify, species are the bricks in the wall, and their loss is inevitably going to weaken the entire ecosystem. Biodiversity is a resource that we can learn to use in a sensible and prudent way and the benefits that can be gained from it are potentially enormous – far greater that the short-term benefits from overexploitation.

6 THREATS TO THE

REEFS

PREVIOUS PAGE: A healthy reef, such as the one this eagle ray is swimming over at Long Cay, Belize, is a prize that we are all working towards.

Threats to reefs are many and varied – although they have always faced stresses from natural factors such as hurricanes, many new ones now affect them, caused by people directly or indirectly. All is not well in these secret underwater cities, and between a third and a half of reefs have been killed in the last half century or so. By understanding the causes of the deaths of these reefs, we can try to prevent and remedy them, but this requires the will to do so. Scientists have already devised solutions by which we can remedy possibly all threats and problems faced by coral reefs, but these solutions require political will, and they often require profound social and economic changes, locally and globally, before they can succeed. Harmful practices of the past

CROWN OF THORNS

The crown of thorns starfish, *Acanthaster planci* (known as 'CoTS'), is one of the biggest causes of coral death in several reefs areas, including the Great Barrier Reef. These starfish grow to about 40 cm (16 in) across and are covered in venomous spines. They eat the coral polyps, digesting them by turning their own stomach inside out and covering the corals with their digestive enzymes. They occur naturally in low numbers on any reef and in this state they are not a problem, but sometimes the population explodes and large numbers of CoTS consume the reef in a very short time. It is not yet understood why these population explosions occur. The trigger is thought to be some form of change in the physical conditions in the habitat – possibly nutrient run-off.

Although it was thought that CoTS were all one species, recent genetic studies have shown that it consists of a species complex, and there may in fact be four distinct species.

ABOVE: The crown of thorns starfish, *Acanthaster planci*, is a natural predator, but the incidence of plague outbreaks is thought to be exacerbated by human actions.

RIGHT: A CoTS infestation that occurred in the British Indian Ocean Territory, an uninhabited and unpolluted marine protected area in the central Indian Ocean. The CoTS grew rapidly in both size and number, devoured most of the coral in that area and then disappeared. It is not known where these starfish go to when they leave a reef area.

that caused the problems in the first place have to be changed – if they *are* changed, there can be greater benefits for all. For example, we must realize that we cannot take an unsustainable amount of fish from the reefs and expect to retain a healthy fish population for the future.

The first step is to recognize that a problem exists. Scientists on their first trip to a coral reef are often overwhelmed by the richness and magnificence of it, yet this reef may be very degraded from what it was 50 years ago. These scientists, however, have no reference against which to judge how rich or how degraded this reef may be, unless they have absorbed a large quantity of older literature. Scientists who have visited the reef before its decline and understand how it should be, know how degraded it has become. This is a human trait known as the 'shifting baseline syndrome', and it is not restricted to coral reefs – there are many examples of this in both the natural and the social worlds. If it is not understood how much a reef has been affected, or indeed if it has been affected at all, it is not possible to improve its condition or work towards restoration of the reef. There will be no knowledge of what it needs to be restored to.

Fisheries are one area where the shifting baseline is evident. No one alive today knows how easy it might have been, or how many fish might have been caught, on a fishing trip 200 years ago. There are some written records, but these are not easy to translate into an image of what a fisher might reasonably be expected to find. Perhaps if we knew exactly what we had lost, we might work harder to regain it.

With approximately 1.36 billion people living within 100 km (62 miles) of tropical shores, it is unsurprising that there are heavy demands on the resources of the reef. The global population is increasing and reefs themselves are becoming degraded, overexploited and therefore less productive, yet the demands on them increase annually. There is migration to the coast too, for many reasons – in the years between 2000 to 2005 the size of the population that lived within 10 km (6 miles) of the coast grew about 30% faster than the average for the rest of the world.

This chapter looks at the loss of the benefits that we obtain from coral reefs that were discussed in the last chapter and considers the impacts that people have had on coral reefs from using them unwisely.

BELOW: With so many people dependant on the resources of the reefs around this island off the coast of Sulawesi, it is unlikely that the reefs will survive the pressure on them, leaving the population with severely reduced resources.

Fisheries

At present coral reef fisheries are carried out at an unsustainable level in most countries with reefs. Modern materials, from nets to boats and engines, allow more efficient fishing and a greater catch, initially at least. While this continues, not only is the total level of fishing unsustainable but the methods used are also damaging to the reef.

Common practices include dynamite fishing, which is very obviously destructive – although it is illegal, it is not uncommon off such coasts as Tanzania and many parts of Southeast Asia. This desperate method of fishing not only removes the fish but also destroys reefs, preventing them from producing the next generation of fish to sustain the fisher and the ecosystem itself. The corals are destroyed and, because many reef fish are herbivores, their removal allows increased growth of macro-algae (seaweeds), which in turn smother the coral. The loss is complex, because if the algae are grazed, they put much of their energy into regrowth. If they are not grazed, when they reach maturity they photosynthesize and produce more organic material than they need, which leaches into the seawater and encourages the growth of microbes, which in turn can cause disease in corals. So the coral is lost, which means the loss of future reef fish and other reef organisms.

RIGHT: Dynamite fishing is surprisingly common in some parts of the world. The practice causes a downward spiral in future fish availability.

CORAL DISEASES

A degree of disease is natural in even a healthy community, but increased levels of disease are a good indication that something is wrong. In relation to coral, the word 'disease' is used in very broad terms and covers anything that negatively affects the health of a coral, from bacterial infection and predation by other organisms, to coral bleaching and pollution.

Predation by other organisms is part of the natural balance of life on a reef, but where extra stressors are put on the reef ecosystem, plague-like epidemics of coral predators can destroy a reef in a very short time. Crown of thorns starfish, corallivorous snails, bristleworms and small coral crabs are known culprits that eat and damage corals. These are always naturally present, and unless stressors stimulate unusual numbers of them they are not a serious danger to healthy corals.

Bacterial, fungal and viral infections are often more serious. These organisms are also often present in seawater without causing any disease, but whenever they increase for any reason, or when there are other stressors on the reef, they may act synergistically (in conjunction with, and enhancing) the disease organisms.

In the 1970s an outbreak of white band disease in the Caribbean killed most of the shallow corals, and since then there have been more outbreaks of this and other diseases throughout the world. The pathogens that cause these diseases do not seem to differ from bacteria that do not cause disease, and sometimes the same bacteria seem to cause different diseases. We still know too little about them. Today several diseases are recognized, including white band disease, black band disease, red band disease, ulcerative white spot, white plague and yellow band disease, among others. White syndrome is a disease that is sweeping coral reefs globally at the moment, and even remote, uninhabited reefs are affected.

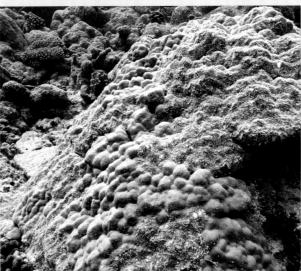

ABOVE LEFT: Many sea fans in the Caribbean, such as this *Gorgonia ventalina*, have been attacked by a fungal disease *Aspergillosis* resulting in the loss of tissue and skeletal material.

ABOVE: Another of the various diseases that are afflicting corals globally. The Caribbean was the first area in which coral disease was recognised as being a serious epidemic.

LEFT: White syndrome disease progressing across an *Acropora* coral. The small greenish patch is live coral; the white is newly dead skeleton; and the large pink and green mottled area has been dead longer and so has a growth of algae covering it.

RIGHT: A sea cucumber, *Holothuria nobilis*, performing the important role of cleaning sand and recycling nutrients on the reef. The sand that has passed through the animal can be seen in the image.

Large fish such as grouper and snapper are valuable, and demand for them from international markets means greater pressure on these species and encourages the poor practices used to catch them. Removal of such top predators from the ecosystem causes a change in the balance between prey and predator, often leading to an increase in the prey species, which then has other impacts on the ecosystem. Human demand is the most significant driver for overfishing, and already more than 80% of the world's shallow coral reefs are severely overfished.

Apart from subsistence fisheries to feed local demand, there is a significant and very lucrative trade in live reef fish for restaurants, primarily for export to Hong Kong and other parts of China. With this trade, fish are caught mainly in Southeast Asia and now extending further into the Pacific and Indian oceans as increasing demand outstrips availability. The demand for specific species – large specimens of fish such as Napoleon wrasse and grouper – means that these top predators are heavily targeted. Demand exceeds supply, so that the stocks have collapsed in most inhabited reef systems in the world.

It is not only fish that are collected from reefs, but many of the species mentioned in Chapter 5 are also taken in commercial quantities, such as octopuses, sea cucumbers and molluscs. Sea cucumbers might not look like very important reef inhabitants, but they perform the crucial function of recycling nutrients and other essential 'housekeeping' functions that keep a reef healthy and productive. Removal of the sea cucumbers has implications beyond their mere loss. They live on the sandy areas of the reef, where they take in sand, digest the organic content, and excrete the now 'clean' sand. Throughout the Indo-Pacific, large numbers of sea cucumbers are taken from reef flats each year – where they are easy to access – and are dried and exported, mainly to Chinese markets.

Aquarium fish trade

Fish are a valuable commercial resource for yet another human use – for stocking the growing number of tropical marine aquaria. It is easy to see why small, beautifully coloured reef fish are popular with aquarists. There is a significant global trade in reef fish, primarily from Southeast Asia, worth over US$300 million a year. Apart from the ecological disruption of removing reef fish from the reef, the initial process of collecting the fish is damaging to the reef. Cyanide is often used to stun the fish, making them easier to collect, but this kills coral polyps or causes them to bleach. Often coral heads are then broken open to extract the stunned fish, which are hidden within them. Although practices have improved, a huge proportion of fish caught for this trade die before they reach the end consumer – which is many of us! The children's film *Finding Nemo* provoked an

LEFT: The regal blue tang, *Paracanthurus hepatus*, is a bright and appealing fish – made popular by the film *Finding Nemo*. It is a very active fish and therefore not well suited to living in an aquarium.

RIGHT: Coral fragments are artificially propagated for both the aquarium trade and reef restoration. Not all species are suitable for popagation, though it works well for some.

increased trade in both anemone fish (which were used for the character of Nemo) and the regal blue tang, *Paracanthurus hepatus* (which was used for the character of Dory), despite the latter being a delicate and difficult species to maintain in an aquarium.

Linked to the removal of fish for marine aquaria is the removal of live coral. It is difficult to imagine that the demand for this material would be sufficient to cause a problem, given the extent of the world's coral reefs. However, aquarists want the most perfect specimens, and to obtain these large areas of reef are sometimes damaged. There is a demand for rare species too, with the detrimental effect that the overcollection of these has on the population. All corals are listed in the Convention on International Trade in Endangered Species (CITES), and special licences are needed to import specimens, but that does not stop people trying, and a couple of hundred colonies are illegally imported and confiscated by customs each year in the UK alone.

In recent years there has been a lot of progress in coral aquaculture, both for the aquarium trade and for reef restoration. For restoration the coral is usually cultivated in special areas *in situ* on a nearby reef area, from fragments that are grown to transplantable size. Although this is certainly a very worthwhile endeavour, it is only going to be able to provide small benefit in global terms. There is also the problem that areas restored by this will have nothing like the diversity of corals that a healthy reef should have, yet people may believe it is a fully restored reef. Corals farmed for the hobby aquarist are usually grown in the country where the demand is located, not where they were originally sourced. This has the benefit that locally grown corals are more likely to survive. However, although that may be good for the coral specimen and the original source reef, it takes away potential income from the people living in the tropical reef areas who need income like this from the reef to encourage them to protect the reef as a valuable resource.

Coral mining

When coral was extracted from a reef to build a few houses for a small population it probably had only a small impact on healthy growing reefs, which could soon recover. Over centuries, many buildings on atolls, for example, have been constructed from corals. However, with growing towns for increasing numbers of people, the amount of coral rock needed as building material, both as rock and as raw limestone for turning into cement, causes a locally severe impact. Malé in the Maldives is a good example of what can happen. In 1986 an estimated 15,000 m^3 (500,000 ft^3) of coral rock was used per annum; no figures are available for today, but it is likely to be significantly more than that.

LEFT: In areas of the world where coral rock is used for building such as here in Malé in the Maldives, increases in town size mean greater demands are made on the reef to provide the materials.

RIGHT: Inshore reefs are often seen as a convenient platform for building upon for coastal development. This of course kills the reef such as these ones here at Jeddah, on the Red Sea coast.

This, along with dredging for sand, has destroyed most of the coral reefs that surround some of the larger islands of this archipelagic nation.

Hand in hand with coral mining is the problem of landfill and coastal development. Reef flats are often considered convenient places to build on. This is sometimes euphemistically termed 'reclamation', although it was never land in the first place. Frequently the material for the landfill is dredged up from nearby reef areas, resulting in the destruction of even more reef. Sediment from a variety of sources, from industry, agriculture and landfill, is very destructive to corals. The sediment blocks out the light needed by the corals and clogs the coral polyps, often completely smothering them. Corals can survive a brief period of turbidity, such as after a storm when heavy rains bring sediment down from rivers, but prolonged sedimentation kills coral reefs in their entirety.

Pollution

With increasing population and material wealth we have an increasing impact on our environment. Oil, pesticides and organic pollutants top the list. But increasingly plastics are becoming a serious problem on reefs and the ocean in general. Large plastic items are unsightly, discarded drinking water bottles being one of the main culprits, but it is when the plastics break down into smaller and smaller pieces that the real problems start. These tiny pieces are termed microplastics and they drift through the water column like plankton. If a piece of this microplastic is ingested by an individual zooplankton it is not digested and provides no nutrition at all. The zooplankton, filled with plankton-sized plastic particles, may then be eaten by a larger organism such as a fish. As a result, the fish accumulates plastic in its gut and dies or suffers reduced growth. Large filter feeders such as manta rays, whale sharks and whales then also accumulate this plastic.

An additional trouble with plastics in the ocean is that pollutants are adsorbed onto the surface of the plastics and are accumulated, so that, when they are eaten they are not only indigestible but also toxic. Large pieces of plastic waste are equally damaging. Piles of plastic on a beach impede turtle nesting. One sad end result of floating plastics is seen in the albatross colony of Midway Atoll in the Pacific, where large numbers of albatross chicks die in the nest having been fed large amounts of plastic, which the parent birds have not been able to distinguish from food.

LEFT: This image shows the terrible consequences of our reckless disposal of our plastic waste. Thousands upon thousands of animals are killed each year by plastic waste, either by eating it or becoming trapped in it.

Global climate change

With an increased amount of carbon dioxide being pumped out as a result of burning fossil fuels, the global atmosphere is warming due to the greenhouse effect. Some of this extra energy, or heat, in the atmosphere is transferred to the oceans, causing them to warm too. Corals live near the upper limit of their thermal tolerance, so this increase in sea temperature stresses them severely. Their symbiotic algae are especially affected, and the corals eject them. When this happens, corals become bleached. Coral bleaching is occurring more and more frequently as the oceans warm. They can survive a short period of this but if it goes on for too long they die. In 1998 about 90% of coral in the Indian Ocean bleached then died after a prolonged warming event, and in the Caribbean in 2005, about a third of shallow corals were killed by warming, most of which has still not recovered. There have been several episodes since then in different parts of the world.

In many places, where there is a collision of climate change stresses with other stresses on corals, the reefs have still have not recovered, as is the case in the Indian Ocean after the 1998 event. In other places where there are few, or no, anthropogenic (human-related) pressures, reefs have recovered from climate change impacts, such as the British Indian Ocean Territory, some of the Maldive Atolls and some of the more

RIGHT: Coral bleaching to this extent is a modern phenomenon caused by warming seawater due to global, man-made, climate change. If the water temperature remains high for too long then all these corals will die.

LEFT: There are other organisms on the reef that have symbiotic zooxanthellae and they can also bleach when the seawater temperature rises. This sea anemone is white because it has lost all its zooxanthellae.

remote Seychelles Atolls. A good analogy of why this is the case would be to image that if you had measles you would most likely survive, but if you had measles, flu, malaria and a salmonella infection all at the same time, your chances of recovery would be much less. It is the same for corals – if they bleach and suffer some sedimentation, pollution and overfishing all at the same time, they do not survive.

When the corals have died the reef can quickly become overgrown with large seaweeds (macro-algae). Once this happens it reduces the chance of corals recovering, as they remain outcompeted by the faster-growing seaweeds, which cover the substrate. Coral larvae cannot attach, and the seaweed shade out any few that do. The reef then becomes an algae-covered substrate, very much lower in biodiversity and of much less value than the healthy coral reef system.

Another consequence of increased atmospheric carbon dioxide is ocean acidification. The carbon dioxide dissolves in water to form carbonic acid. Acids dissolve carbonate, and it has been shown that coral growth slows down with only a very small rise in acidity. Carbon dioxide dissolves more readily in cold water, so the acidification is happening first in the colder waters at higher latitudes. Many important species of plankton, such as pteropods and diatoms, have been found to be highly susceptible to acidification, as have corals.

A third consequence of climate change is that of sea level rise. The huge ice deposits at the poles and in mountain glaciers are melting alarmingly, adding more water to the oceans. At the same time, the warming is causing thermal expansion of the oceans because warm water takes up more space than cold water, in the same way as other materials expand when heated. A substantial proportion of sea level rise is due to this factor alone. If the rate of rise is slow enough, healthy coral reefs may be able to grow to keep up with it. But coral islands are low lying, many being only a metre or two above sea level, and they may not survive the rising waters if the reef growth is diminished by other factors at the same time.

Loving reefs to death

More and more tourists are visiting coral reefs, where swimming, snorkelling, diving or just having a beach holiday are popular activities. But walking on a reef breaks coral and can cause a lot of damage, especially in busy tourist resorts. Careless snorkelers and divers can also break the coral, and fins of inexperienced divers are commonly the cause of much breakage. The taking of coral souvenirs, shells and other reef items causes a large amount of destruction, too.

RIGHT: The danger of showing the beauty and magnificence of coral reefs is that it encourages tourists to go and see for themselves. While this has many benefits, too many people can then become a different problem.

Boats that are used to take tourists and divers to visit the reef can cause much damage. Anchors dropped carelessly on the reef damage a lot of coral every year and if the boat swings on a heavy chain attached to the anchor it can destroy a large swathe of coral. Like most things there is a solution to this and the use of permanent moorings is becoming more common, especially in marine parks.

Coastal infrastructure, such as hotels and harbours can also have an impact on the coral reefs. It must make sense to local developers though, not to kill the goose that lays the golden egg! Although the 'ecotourism' label is often misused, careful planning in consultation with ecologists can help minimise any damage.

It is not just one factor that is damaging reefs, but the combined assault from many things. Pollution and overfishing may be locally most important in many places but climate change causing warming seawater and acidification are the biggest long-term threats of all. If carbon dioxide discharges continue at the rate they now are doing, in the end this will destroy even those reefs that are well managed and protected.

To date, about a half of the world's coral reefs have been destroyed in the last half a century, and more are under serious threat of destruction and are already in a degraded state. For example, shockingly, the Great Barrier Reef has lost half of its corals in the past 27 years. The global rate of decline of reefs is increasing, and it is estimated that they are disappearing at the rate of 1–2% every year – twice the speed of rainforests.

Reefs are critical for all sorts of reasons. If we are to save them we need to act fast.

CONSERVATION

PREVIOUS PAGE: Evolving technology is allowing marine scientists new and more efficient ways to gather field data from coral reefs. Pictured here is the Catlin Seaview Survey's SVII camera on Glovers Reef, Belize.

The story of coral reefs has been a rollercoaster ride. Following widespread use of scuba equipment, the startling discovery of such an incredible wealth of biodiversity was stunning. Had we been able to see coral reefs in their entirely pristine state several decades earlier, we would have been even more amazed. Now, although there are still many wonderful reefs in the world, they are becoming fewer and more degraded with each passing year. In 2009 a Coral Crisis meeting of some of the world's top marine scientists was held at the Royal Society to highlight the danger to coral reefs of global atmospheric carbon dioxide levels exceeding 350 parts per million (ppm), and of the rapid and terminal decline of reefs if levels were to be allowed to reach 450 ppm. At that point reefs will cease to have their current value to humanity. By 2013 the level had exceeded 400 ppm! What can we do? Is the demise of these wonderful places inevitable?

No hope?

When we realize how much damage has been done to coral reef habitats, and what demands are still being made of them, it would be easy to write them off and think that little can be done to save them. Indeed, many reef scientists already believe that little can be done, and that reefs are already doomed. A question often asked of coral reef conservationists who are trying to protect and conserve reefs, even when they might believe that there is no hope for them, is: Why bother if there is no hope? One answer to that question is that even someone with a terminal illness goes to the doctor in the

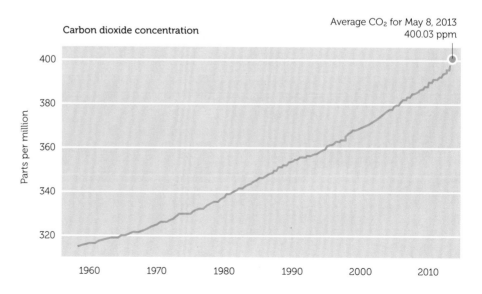

Carbon dioxide concentration

Average CO_2 for May 8, 2013
400.03 ppm

RIGHT: Graph showing the increase in atmospheric carbon dioxide in the last 55 years – an increase from 320 to 400 ppm.

hope of a cure or something to extend or ease their life. Even the most pessimistic coral reef biologists find it difficult to truly believe that we could destroy these huge, rich and biodiverse places in such a short time. Yet it is not quite true that there is absolutely no hope for coral reefs. As mentioned in Chapter 6, reef ecologists have solutions for the issues that are affecting the reefs. Lack of knowledge is not the problem – the problem is lack of political will to apply it. Yet we need to do so, because so many people depend on reefs for so much. Although climate change effects are so pervasive, there is abundant scientific evidence to show that healthy reefs that do not suffer any additional anthropogenic stresses such as pollution are more resilient to it, and are more likely to recover from spells of warming that cause them to bleach or even die.

Marine protected areas

One obvious answer is to protect as many of the world's reefs as we can from local impacts such as pollution and overfishing in the hope that a solution will be found in time to solve the problems caused by the rise in atmospheric carbon dioxide. In areas where local communities rely on the resources of their reefs, careful management strategies have to be put in place to allow the resources to be used while at the same time allowing damaged

LEFT: A healthy crop of juvenile corals colonising a dead *Acropora* table. Turnover is natural on a reef and where there are no external stressors on the reef it can recover remarkably quickly.

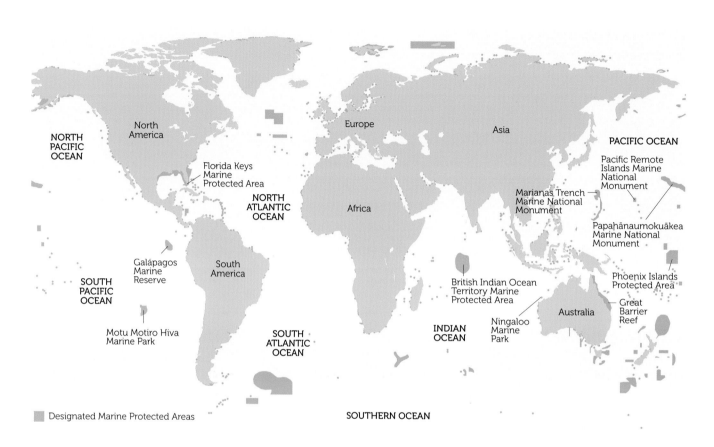

NORTH PACIFIC OCEAN

North America

Europe

Asia

PACIFIC OCEAN

Pacific Remote Islands Marine National Monument

Florida Keys Marine Protected Area

NORTH ATLANTIC OCEAN

Africa

Marianas Trench Marine National Monument

Papahānaumokuākea Marine National Monument

Galápagos Marine Reserve

South America

SOUTH PACIFIC OCEAN

British Indian Ocean Territory Marine Protected Area

Phoenix Islands Protected Area

Motu Motiro Hiva Marine Park

SOUTH ATLANTIC OCEAN

INDIAN OCEAN

Ningaloo Marine Park

Australia

Great Barrier Reef

Designated Marine Protected Areas

SOUTHERN OCEAN

ABOVE: The targets to protect 10% of the ocean by 2020 are unlikely to be met at the present rate of protection. Not all the MPAs on this map are effective, as many allow various extractive activities, such as fishing, to be undertaken.

reefs to recover. In areas where corals have died and where the stressor has then been removed, careful management may allow new coral growth on the old, dead coral.

Areas like this are called marine protected areas (MPAs), or marine managed areas (MMAs). These come in all shapes, sizes and degrees of effectiveness. Merely declaring something to be protected does not make it so, no more than saying that you are on a diet yet continuing to eat as before makes you lose weight. It is the same with MPAs, merely declaring an area to be protected without the scientific information needed to manage it, and without effective enforcement of that protection, provides no benefit. Such areas are called 'paper parks', that is a park in name only. There are too many of those in the world.

The most effective MPAs in terms of conservation are those that are fully no-take – in other words, nothing may be removed from them. Where there is a local community that is dependent on the reef, this is obviously difficult; the local people need to be able to support themselves. Most MPAs allow a carefully managed level of fishing, and although local people may be concerned that they will be unable to catch all that they need, time and again research has shown that with careful management more fish and other extractive resources become available after only a short time. Incomes rise too. Where a fisher previously had to fish for six hours to feed his family, within a properly managed area he might fish for less time to catch the same amount. The problems come when some want to remove more, because more becomes available, a course of action that then leads back to the depleted state in a very short time.

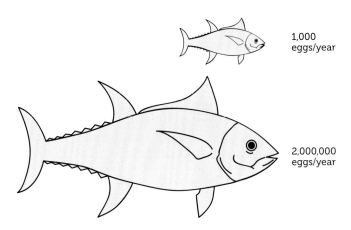

1,000
eggs/year

2,000,000
eggs/year

ABOVE: Catching the big ones and letting the small ones go is normal fisheries policy. This does not make sense for increasing fish stocks.

If a well-managed area that allows a carefully controlled fishery is located next to a no-take MPA, the benefits are increased because of a spill-over effect. But no matter how well managed, an area cannot provide more than it is naturally capable of doing.

A small fish usually produces a much smaller number of young each year than does a large adult of the same species. A common fishery management strategy is to allow the fisher to take only the larger fish and to return the small ones. Ideally, we should be leaving many large specimens too, as they are the ones that produce most young. In a no-take MPA, fish are able to grow large and produce many young, which themselves grow up to maturity. Some of this increased population stay to breed another generation and some move out of the no-take MPA to 'spill over' into the adjoining managed area, resulting in an even better fishery for the local community.

There are some who oppose MPAs – commonly individuals or groups who have vested interests in using and exploiting the resources of the reefs and who would lose out if it was protected. Some commercial fisheries might have this view. Others might criticize MPAs as being 'fortress conservation' for excluding local people. But when MPAs bring benefits to local people and their environment, such conservation is difficult to argue against.

The Decade of Biodiversity

The United Nations Convention on Biological Diversity has declared the present decade to 2020 to be the Decade of Biodiversity. A list of internationally recognized and ratified targets known as the Aichi targets have been set. Aichi target 11 calls for 10% of the ocean

CASE HISTORY – The British Indian Ocean Territory Marine Protected Area

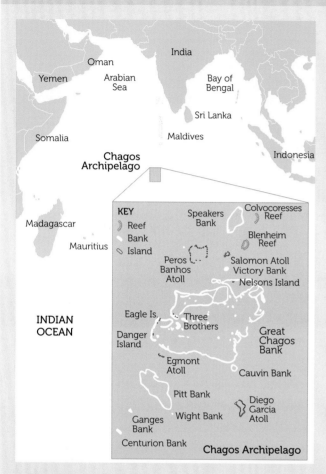

LEFT: Map showing the Chagos Archipelago, a British overseas territory in the Indian Ocean that was declared a fully no-take Marine Protected Area (MPA) in 2010.

BELOW: With no human impacts, the reefs of Chagos are some of the healthiest and most productive in the world.

for 45 years, so there have been almost no anthropogenic pressures on them for a long time. The key difference the declaration made to the territory was that the industrial tuna fishing fleet was excluded from fishing the waters. This created a sanctuary for tuna species that were heavily fished globally, along with the accompanying by-catch.

Chagos was probably no different to most other Indian Ocean reefs prior to the 1980s, but after the 1998 Indian Ocean-wide warming event that killed 90% of corals, the Chagos reefs were killed down to considerable depths, just like the rest of the Indian Ocean reefs. However, because Chagos suffers no other anthropogenic stresses, the reefs recovered well. By 2006 coral cover was back to about half its original level, and by 2012 had returned to its pre-warming level, unlike many of the other reefs in the Indian Ocean, which suffered from issues such as sewage discharges, sand mining and overfishing. As a result of the good health of the reefs and the lack of fishing pressure on them, not only did the coral recover quickly but also the biomass of reef fish there is many times higher than any other place in the Indian Ocean. Chagos, as an important reservoir of intact and unspoilt reefs, is in a position to provide larvae of very many species to help repopulate the seriously depleted reefs down current in the western Indian Ocean.

The reefs of Chagos are also important as a natural laboratory. So many other reefs suffer from a variety of impacts that it is difficult for scientists to know if measurements are the result of natural causes or other influences. In Chagos, where there are no other influences, valuable baseline data on how a healthy reef should function is collected. The MPA produces benefits for its numerous coral islands, too. The Chagos islands are the most important places in the Indian Ocean for breeding seabirds, and several endangered species from turtles to the giant coconut crab have a refuge there too.

The British Indian Ocean Territory, also known as the Chagos Archipelago, is a group of five atolls and several offshore banks in the middle of the Indian Ocean. The area has been the subject of decades of scientific research and is one of the best-understood places in the Indian Ocean. The inhabitants were brought to the islands to work on copra plantations and moved back to Mauritius in the 1960s, after the decline of the global copra trade, in order to make way for a US military establishment on the southernmost of the five atolls, Diego Garcia. Most of its atolls have been uninhabited since then.

In 2010 the UK government, after a period of public consultation, designated the entire 650,000 km² (251,000 miles²) out to the 200-mile limit to be a fully no-take marine protected area (MPA). Diego Garcia and a 3 km (1.9 mile) strip surrounding the atoll are excluded from the MPA. Chagos is the biggest fully no-take MPA in the world – some MPAs are larger but are not fully no-take. These atolls have been uninhabited to become protected by 2020, and that would be a very important step which may allow some reefs to withstand the current assault. Unfortunately, at present rates of creation, this target will not be reached in time.

One interesting result of the ocean warming as a result of climate change is that some corals are migrating to higher latitudes, for example in Japan the recent colonization by *Acropora hyacinthus* is thought to be due to ocean warming. Some people are hopeful that this might provide a small refuge for corals. Regions where this is expected to occur are Bermuda, South Africa, southeastern Australia and as the example above, Japan. The species that do this will no doubt last longer than those that do not, but only a small number of species are likely to migrate and the new reef communities will not have anything like the biodiversity of present reefs. As ocean acidification is affecting higher latitudes first and working towards the lower latitudes, these migrating corals are likely to be affected by this factor earlier. This has been termed the 'nutcracker effect': the squeezing of reefs between the increased acidity at higher latitudes and the increasing temperature exceeding coral tolerances near the equator.

Conserving reefs is no longer a biological, scientific problem. We know enough to do that now. Rather, it is a problem of, and for, society and politics. What can people do? Quite simply it is in the power of individuals to persuade governments to create more protected areas for reefs. Also, we must control and eliminate pollution, greatly decrease carbon dioxide emissions by developing sustainable energy, reduce destructive shoreline activities and stop overfishing. If nature has a chance to do so, it can restore itself. Indeed allowing it to do so is usually far better than trying to 'manage' it back to health. We need to give reefs a chance.

Many countries, not only primarily tropical ones, have extensive coral reefs. The UK, the USA, France and the Netherlands are responsible, through their overseas territories, for huge tracts of coral reefs in all three tropical oceans. Canvass your government representative, write to the papers, make your feelings known. There are many conservation groups that you can join who are working in this field and who can help make your voice louder by bringing like-minded people together. In the words of F. Scott Fitzgerald, 'The test of a first rate intelligence is the ability ... to be able to see that things are hopeless and yet be determined to make them otherwise.'

THE CATLIN SEAVIEW SURVEY

The Catlin Seaview Survey, sponsored by international insurer Catlin Group Limited, is a series of scientific expeditions that encompasses the first comprehensive attempt to document the composition and health of the world's coral reefs. The Survey accomplishes this goal by capturing unprecedented 3-D panoramic images of reef systems, which allow scientists to study the reefs no matter where they are based.

As an insurance and reinsurance company. Catlin is in the business of helping its clients manage all types of risks and threats. While insurers know a great deal about the risks their clients currently face, surprisingly little is known about the risks that future generations may encounter, especially risks emanating from climate change and other changes to our planet.

The goal of the Catlin Seaview Survey is to improve scientists' understanding of the future of our planet, particularly its oceans, through the collection of reliable, impartial scientific data. By sponsoring activities such as the Catlin Seaview Survey, Catlin believes it can help its clients – and the entire global community – to learn more about the Earth and the risks that our children and grandchildren must manage.

Catlin began its support for environmental research in 2009 when it commenced the Catlin Arctic Survey, a three-year series of scientific expeditions to examine impact of climate change and other factors on the ecologically fragile Arctic environment. As a result of the data collected by the Catlin Arctic Survey, some scientists now believe that the Arctic Ocean could be ice-free during summers within a decade, significantly earlier than the majority of previous computer-based models had previously projected.

After three years of sponsoring research in the bitterly cold Arctic, Catlin re-focused its efforts on a very different feature of the Earth's environment, the coral reefs found primarily in tropical locations. Coral habitats, like the Arctic, serve as early-warning systems for significant changes occurring to our oceans. The disappearance of coral reefs could potentially affect the livelihoods of millions of people and have grave consequences for tourism, aquaculture and pharmaceutical research.

The Catlin Seaview Survey has been a truly global research project. During 2012, the Survey focused on the Great Barrier Reef off Australia, the world's largest coral reef system. The 2013 Survey explored the myriad coral reefs of the Caribbean and the coral reefs off Bermuda, which is Catlin's headquarters. Activities in 2014 were centred on the 'Coral Triangle' of the Western Pacific Ocean, while the 2015 Survey is scheduled to concentrate on the reefs found in the Indian Ocean and the Red Sea.

Much of the research conducted by the Catlin Seaview Survey has been done at relatively shallow depths of 30 m (98 ft) or less. Typically, this type of survey can be conducted by a single diver using the SVII camera system that was specially designed for the Catlin Seaview Survey (see page 106).

During selected expeditions, the team also studies the mesophotic zone or 'deep reefs', from approximately 30 to 100 m (98 to 328 ft) in depth through the use of remotely operated vehicles (ROV). These ROVs are fitted with custom remote-controlled DSLR cameras to record high-definition, wide-angle video, aided by a 20,000+ lumen lighting system to illuminate the murky ocean depths. The ROVs also carefully collect coral specimens from

BELOW: A deep diving remotely operated vehicle (ROV). Scientists use the ROV to collect data from the mesophotic zone, between depths of 30–100 m (98–328 ft). These are depths that are unsafe for divers to visit on scuba.

THE SVII CAMERA

The Catlin Seaview Survey's SVII camera has revolutionized underwater research. The SVII, which can be piloted by a single diver assisted by a tablet computer, is able to take rapid-fire 360° images at an interval of 3 seconds while traveling at a speed of approximately 4 km/h. Images are then stitched together and can be published online in a fashion that allows anyone with a desktop, laptop, tablet or smartphone to self-navigate a 'virtual dive' in stunning high-resolution.

For each image captured, a geo-location and camera direction is also recorded, meaning it's possible to retake the photograph at a later date from the exact same camera position as the original.

BELOW: The SVII camera captures high-resolution 360° panoramic imagery which is used by scientists and marine park managers to study change on the coral reef over time. Pictured here is the SVII camera on the incredibly biodiverse reef system of the Coral Triangle, Indonesia.

these depths to allow scientists to determine their genetic make-up. The Catlin Seaview Survey now possesses the largest collection of mesophotic corals in the world.

One of the cornerstones of the Catlin Seaview Survey is the necessity to share the images with the wider scientific community. To facilitate this, the Catlin Global Reef Record has been established as a research tool that collates and communicates the coral reef science produced by the Catlin Seaview Survey, including hundreds of thousands of images, and combines that information with data from other leading sources of ocean research. The Catlin Global Reef Record provides scientists across various disciplines of marine studies with a means to analyze the current state of the reef ecosystems on a local, regional and global scale and to monitor changes that occur over time.

While the general public can view the breathtaking images of the world's coral reefs via the Catlin Global Reef Record, anyone with access to the internet can take a 'virtual dive' to discover the beauty of scores of coral reefs worldwide through a partnership between the Catlin Seaview Survey and Google Maps. Using a personal computer or a tablet, one can share the experience of navigating along a coral reef.

The Catlin Seaview Survey is directed by Underwater Earth, a not-for-profit agency based in Sydney, Australia, that is focused on the communication of ocean issues. The Survey's lead science partner is the Global Change Institute (GCI) at The University of Queensland, Australia. Professor Ove Hoegh-Guldberg, the GCI's Director, serves as Chief Scientist of the Catlin Seaview Survey. He and a team of marine biologists identify the survey sites and then assist in carrying out all survey work, ensuring that specific scientific methodologies are followed at all times. In addition to the images captured by the Survey, Professor Hoegh-Guldberg and his team are also writing a series of scientific papers that will report detailed observations from the Survey's activities.

More information about the Catlin Seaview Survey is available at:
www.CatlinSeaviewSurvey.com and www.Catlin.com/SeaviewSurvey

The Catlin Global Reef Record is located at:
www.CatlinGlobalReefRecord.org

Anyone can take a virtual dive with the Catlin Seaview Survey at:
www.google.com/maps/views/streetview/oceans

INDEX

FURTHER INFORMATION

GENERAL CORAL REEF ECOLOGY AND CONSERVATION

Roberts C., *The Unnatural History of the Sea*. Gaia Books Ltd., 2007, 448 pp.

Rowher F. and Youle M., *Coral Reefs in the Microbial Seas. Plaid Press*, 2010, 204 pp.

Sheppard C.R.C., *Coral Reefs*. Colin Baxter Photography Ltd., 2002, 72 pp.

Sheppard C.R.C. *Coral Reefs: A Very Short Introduction*. Oxford University Press, 2014, 144 pp.

Sheppard C.R.C., Davy S., Pilling G., *Biology of Coral Reefs*. Oxford University Press, 2009, 339 pp.

Spalding M., Ravilious C., Green E.P., *Atlas of Coral Reefs*. University of California Press, 2001, 425 pp.

Stone G.S. and Obura D., *Underwater Eden: Saving the Last Coral Wilderness on Earth*. The University of Chicago Press, 2013, 160 pp.

Veron J.E.N., *Corals in Space and Time. The biogeography and evolution of the Scleractinia*. UNSW Press, 1995, 321 pp.

Veron J.E.N., *A Reef in Time: the Great Barrier Reef from Beginning to End*. Harvard University Press. 2007, 207 pp.

Wilkinson C.R., *Status of Coral Reefs of the World: 2008*. Global Coral Reef Monitoring Network and Reef and Rainforest Research Centre, Townsville, 2008, pp. 298.

Zell L., *The Great Barrier Reef*. Murdoch Books, 2012, 256 pp.

IDENTIFICATION GUIDES

Allen G.R. and Steene R., *Indo Pacific Coral Reef Field Guide*. Tropical Reef Research, 2007, 378 pp.

Fabricius K and Alderslade P., *Soft Corals and Sea Fans*. Australian institute of Marine Science, 2001, 264 pp.

Humann P. and Deloach N., *The Reef Set: Your Eyes to the Sea-Reef Fish, Creature Coral Identification*, (3 vols). New World Publications, 2002, 1250 pp.

Kelly R., *Coral Finder Indo Pacific*. BYO Guides, 2009, 30 pp.

Lieske E. and Myers R., *Coral Reef Fishes*. Princeton University Press, 2001, 400 pp.

Lieske E. and Myers R., *Coral Reef Guide Red Sea*. Collins, 2004, 384 pp.

Richmond M.D., ed. *A Guide to the Seashores of Eastern Africa and the Western Indian Ocean Islands*. SIDA, 1997, 448 pp.

Veron J.E.N., *Corals of the World*, (3 vols). Australian Institute of Marine Science, 2000, 1350 pp.

WEBSITES

About Corals
http://coral.aims.gov.au

British Indian Ocean Territory Marine Protected Area
http://chagos-trust.org

Coralpedia – Your guide to Caribbean corals and sponges
http://coralpedia.bio.warwick.ac.uk

Great Barrier Reef
http://www.gbrmpa.gov.au/about-the-reef/facts-about-the-great-barrier-reef

NOAA Coral Reef Information System
http://www.coris.noaa.gov

Ocean Portal
http://ocean.si.edu/corals-and-coral-reefs

The Big Ocean Managers Network
http://bigoceanmanagers.org

NB. Websites are correct at time of publication.

ACKNOWLEDGEMENTS

My husband Charles Sheppard has always inspired and encouraged me, both in marine biology and with underwater photography. He is the reason that I was able to write this book, thank you Charles.

I would also like to thank three groups for enabling diving at some lovely locations to take many of the photographs: Dive Ningaloo in Exmouth, Australia; Roctopus Dive in Koh Tao, Thailand; and the Chagos Conservation Trust for the British Indian Ocean Territory.

A thank you is also due to all the marine conservationists who are working to try to protect our oceans. And I would like to thank the managers of all the Marine Protected Areas, the world needs you all.

PICTURE CREDITS